The Next Big Thing

THE DALTON CAMP LECTURES IN JOURNALISM

THE NEXT BIG THING

Edited by
PHILIP LEE

GOOSE LANE

Cover and page design by Chris Tompkins.
Cover photo by Jusben (www.morguefile.com/creative/Jusben).
Printed in Canada.
10 9 8 7 6 5 4 3 2 1

Library and Archives Canada Cataloguing in Publication

The next big thing : the Dalton Camp Lectures in Journalism
/ edited by Philip Lee.

Co-published by: St. Thomas University.
Issued in print and electronic formats.
ISBN 978-0-86492-348-6 (pbk.). — ISBN 978-0-86492-729-3 (epub)

1. Journalism — Canada. 2. Journalism. I. Lee, Philip J., 1963-,
editor II. St. Thomas University (Fredericton, N.B.)

PN4909.N49 2014   070.40971   C2014-903800-3
C2014-903801-1

Goose Lane Editions acknowledges the generous support of the Canada Council for the Arts, the Government of Canada through the Canada Book Fund (CBF), and the Government of New Brunswick through the Department of Tourism, Heritage and Culture.

Goose Lane Editions
500 Beaverbrook Court, Suite 330
Fredericton, New Brunswick
CANADA E3B 5X4
www.gooselane.com

For June Callwood and Neil Reynolds

CONTENTS

INTRODUCTION
A Small Drop of Ink

I became friends with Dalton Camp during my last tour in the newspaper business when I was editor-in-chief of the New Brunswick *Telegraph-Journal*. One morning soon after I took the job, Dalton called to ask for a lunch meeting and suggested the dining room at the Hilton Hotel on the Saint John waterfront. When I arrived, Dalton was seated and had ordered a bottle of red wine. He poured me a glass.

It was a long lunch, and the start of a conversation that continued until Dalton died. That day we talked about New Brunswick politics, my plans for the newspaper, and Dalton's national column, which we published twice a week in syndication from the *Toronto Star*. I asked if he would consider writing an exclusive column about New Brunswick politics for us. We agreed on a price, and Camp's column started arriving by fax Sunday evenings for Monday morning's paper.

We landed Canada's best political writer at a time when he had a lot to write about. The provincial Liberals had been in power for more than a decade since the Tories, led by Dalton's old friend Richard Hatfield, had been destroyed at the polls in 1987. Frank McKenna, the premier and architect of the 58-0 victory and two subsequent majority governments, had stepped down and his successor, Camille Thériault, was stumbling. Some Liberals had started to believe they were entitled to govern in perpetuity. Camp wrote that this happens to all political parties, that over time they mistake their good for the public good and this contributes to their downfall. In June 1999, a young Tory leader named Bernard Lord won a landslide victory over the Liberals.

A year later, Richard Myers, the vice-president academic at St. Thomas University in Fredericton, asked me if I would be interested in teaching and building a journalism program at his university. I left the daily newspaper business and began a new career.

I left newspapers just as a digital revolution was sweeping through our profession, changing both the economic model and the craft of journalism — and it's not over yet. Print advertising, which for a century paid for editorial content and made newspaper owners rich, was fragmenting and moving online. Newspapers moved their content online, but advertisers didn't stay with them. Hundreds of newspapers with long and successful histories closed. Those that survived have yet to find a new economic model that works as well as the old one.

The craft of reporting and telling stories with words and pictures and printing them on paper, or writing and editing a television or radio news story for an evening newscast, now involves multimedia production, social media management, and getting information online fast enough to capture a fickle audience that has a vast menu of information available around the clock.

We've all been running so hard to keep up that it's been difficult to take stock of what's been gained and lost. We no longer need a printing press to publish, or a transmitter to broadcast. This is a good thing for the free expression of ideas. We now have access to vast amounts of information, which is useful for reporting, and the walls that once concealed state secrets have crumbled, which is a victory for open societies.

This is also the best of times for anyone with an opinion. There's even a new shorthand language for instant opinions:

Like it? Thumbs up.

Digg?

Trending?

Click.

Comment.

Instagram.

Tweet. Retweet.

\#

:) :(

Most of the journalists I know are immersed in the instanews environment. They have no choice. In a world where all opinions are created
equal, what matters is to be fast and first. There's nothing wrong with
fast and first. Journalists have been playing that game a long time. But
there's a difference when we define fast and first as right now rather than
as an evening newscast or tomorrow morning's newspaper. We report
the latest developments in stories before we understand the stories ourselves. The best journalists have never played that game before. And just
because technology allows us to do something doesn't make it good, or
right, or true.

What I know from my experience is that finding the right words to tell
true stories can change the world in ways big and small. The stories that
matter often come to us in the quiet moments, in the world of slow time.

Dalton Camp's memoir, *Gentlemen, Players and Politicians* tells the
story of the night of the 1952 New Brunswick election. Camp had engineered
a victory for Hugh John Flemming's Tories, outwitting Liberal adman
Richard O'Hagan, and when the victory parties were over he retired to
his room in Fredericton's Lord Beaverbrook Hotel. In the silence of the
night, he looked out his window, saw the blinking lights on the railway
bridge spanning the St. John River and thought of Bryan Priestman, a
war veteran and physics professor at the University of New Brunswick.
Seven years earlier, on Remembrance Day, the professor had died trying
to save an eight-year-old boy from drowning.

Priestman was taking a shortcut across the bridge, as was his habit,
when the boy, who was walking with a friend, slipped through the tracks
and dropped into the water. Priestman didn't hesitate. He took off his
jacket and hat and jumped off the side of the bridge. He reached the boy
but couldn't bring him to shore. Either the current was too strong or they
got tangled around a pier, no one knows for sure. Fire fighters and police
found the bodies the next morning, the man's arms still wrapped around
the boy.

"I am never able to look at the bridge without thinking of Priestman, whoever he was, and having thought of him again, the mind becomes reflective, turning to politics, and, on this occasion, the evening's celebration of the mindless, easy victory, the self-satisfaction suddenly touched by introspection, the wine turning sour," Camp wrote. "Hugh John Flemming, thirty-seven, Austin Taylor, fifteen. Dalton Camp, thirty-seven, Richard O'Hagan, fifteen. New Brunswick thirty-seven, New Brunswick, fifteen. Bryan Priestman, zero."

Camp looked out across the river in the night and recognized that in the bloodless wars of politics even the best of us sacrifice ideals for the ambitions of others. Meanwhile, moral choices that require real acts of courage are right there in front of us, on every bridge we cross. In this life, the most honest words we write are those that require courage. Dalton understood that there's a lot at stake, and honest words don't come easy.

One evening, several years after I left the *Telegraph-Journal*, my wife Deb Nobes and I met Dalton Camp for dinner. He was living in a Fredericton hotel, trying to complete his memoirs. He knew he didn't have time to waste. Almost a decade earlier he had been the oldest Canadian to undergo a successful heart transplant. That night he was feeling old, shuffling through the carpeted corridors in his slippers. We sat in the bar and had dinner brought to us there. He drank red wine, ate soup and ice cream, and spoke about the book, how he was stuck, struggling to find the right words to say what he needed to say, struggling to be honest with himself.

A few days later, he suffered a stroke. I walked up the hill from the university to visit him in the hospital. One day, he had his typewriter perched on his lap in bed. He knew he was running out of time. He was released from hospital but soon suffered another stroke. He died on March 18, 2002.

One afternoon that spring, I called Bernie Lucht, the longtime executive producer of CBC Radio's *Ideas*, a program I admired. I asked Lucht if *Ideas* would be interested in producing a lecture series in partnership with St. Thomas University called the Dalton Camp Lecture in Journalism that over time would create a public conversation about the role of journalism in society. We would host the lectures and the *Ideas* team would come to Fredericton and record them for broadcast on the show. I expected Lucht to take the proposal away and think about it for awhile. Instead, he agreed to the partnership and during that phone call we settled on terms that remain in place to this day.

In October 2002, June Callwood came to our campus and delivered the first Camp lecture to a standing-room-only crowd. *Ideas* host Paul Kennedy moderated the event. Lucht, who I hadn't met before our first phone conversation, came to Fredericton, fussed over the recording from the front row, and became a new friend of the university, eventually joining us for a semester as a visiting professor.

The Camp lecture series has been a remarkable project. The formula is simple, defined by Lucht's genius for how to make good radio: we hold one meeting a year to choose journalists who we think have something to say and we let them talk about what they want to talk about for an hour in front of an engaged audience of students and members of the community. It has been a fascinating journey, and in many ways the most successful and satisfying project of my professional life.

From the beginning we planned one day to collect the lectures into a book. Now, twelve years into the project, we have decided it is time. What we have is a collection of reports from the field from journalists who have been working through this period of profound change, as the next big thing waits just around the corner. What is remarkable about this collection is the optimism of our speakers. What interests them is how we can continue to tell the stories that change the world.

Several years after Dalton died, Deb and I took our young daughter Lucy to Robertson's Point on Grand Lake about half an hour from Fredericton for the weekend. We borrowed a cottage from our friend Michael, Dalton's son, who teaches with me at St. Thomas University. Dalton loved Robertson's Point and the lush fields and forests along the lake and down the St. John River valley.

On Saturday morning I woke early to work and sat at a writing desk by a bay window. Underneath the desk I found stacks of Camp's columns, which years earlier had been written on his typewriter and faxed from the cottage to editors at the *Toronto Star*. When he was finished answering questions from the editors on the telephone, he must have tossed the pages there and fittingly there beneath the desk they remained.

The columns were typed on Dalton's manual typewriter then heavily revised with a pen, words scratched out and replaced, sentences rewritten in the margins. I remembered this was the way his New Brunswick column came in on the fax machine when I was editing the newspaper. Camp's column never made it into the digital age.

He used to say that in the struggle to find the right words he would discover what he really thought. What he thought mattered and he knew it, so he took the time to find the words to say what he needed to say. For a long time, I read his words in the silence of early morning as the sunrise warmed my back.

Lord Byron wrote that words are things, and a small drop of ink produces that which makes thousands, perhaps millions think.

I spend too much time surrounded by smart young people to wring my hands and say we won't ever get it right. It's just that some days I fear we are rushing forward so fast in this new instanews environment that we will forget how to slow down long enough to find the right words to tell the stories that need to be told.

How will we continue to value words in an inkless world? I hope the lectures we have collected here, and those we will collect in another edition down the road, will help to answer this question.

JUNE CALLWOOD
The Best Game in Town

We will always be grateful to June Callwood for beginning this lecture series with a grace, style, and enthusiasm that set the standard for all that followed. She came to campus after a long and storied career in journalism and social activism in Canada, a writer of magazine stories and books, a television host, the founder of a home for people dying of AIDS. We put up posters and waited to see what would happen. That evening our 140-seat lecture hall filled, and there was still a lineup out into the courtyard. She invited students to come and sit on the stage at her feet. She told them her knees might look cute but they weren't worth a damn. June Callwood died on April 14, 2007.

It's customary to begin a lecture named for an esteemed person by acknowledging that it is a great honour. I don't think those acknowledgements are ever perfunctory but I'm especially delighted and grateful to be chosen to give the first Dalton Camp Lecture in Journalism. Stunned comes closer to the truth. I try not to think what Dalton might be saying about this. He and I were friends for a long time indeed and we were comrades in many struggles involving civil liberties, but my appointment to give the first lecture in the series named for him might stretch his tolerance for upstarts to the snapping point. I don't think Dalton and I ever had a conversation where we found ourselves in fundamental disagreement but we always seemed to arrive at the same place by different directions.

I watched Dalton through many changes during his distinguished life and he affirmed for me my theory that most people invent themselves. At some point in their lives people are inclined to pause and consider the stew of experiences and the gene pool that fix their range of behavioural possibilities. They feel a need to know what they will not allow themselves to do, at least not without profound remorse, and how they like to see themselves performing. In the teens or twenties or whenever bouts of self-examination begin, an individual's code of conduct needs to be written in pencil in order to facilitate revisions. But eventually over the trials and the follies of a developing person, behaviour is shaped more or less permanently by a set of ethical principles one hopes will stand up in bad weather. The existential question for every human is what is the point? For instance, Gandhi decided one day, sitting tranquilly under a tree, that his reason for being on earth was to oppose injustice, untruth, and humbug. My own theology is still a work in progress but I like to think there is divinity and kindness.

People sometimes joke that Dalton Camp had two cracks at defining the meaning of his life since he was a man who had two hearts. If so, he got it right both times. He said in the foreword to his first book, *Gentlemen, Players and Politicians*, a wise and charming memoir about his early years in politics, that Canadians don't bestride the world like a colossus. That role is taken by you-know-who south of us. Instead we are a people of small huts, clusters of neighbourhoods, keepers of modest gardens. Dalton went on to say, "So what is recorded for our posterity is not the chronicle of awesome events but the memory of how individuals responded to personal crisis, challenge and opportunity. How power affected them, how low they would stoop or how tall they would stand in order to conquer." I would add that the conquest of which he spoke was not a victory over others but the private triumph of maintaining a level of personal decency. Now Vaclav Havel, the writer who was imprisoned for his heroic defiance of oppression in what was Czechoslovakia, wrote some years ago that our main enemy today is our own bad traits: which he said were indifference to the common good, vanity, personal ambition, selfishness, and rivalry. Dalton Camp possessed not one of those sour attributes.

Dalton slid into journalism edgewise and rather late in life, unlike the journalism students in this hall tonight. He didn't really plan to end his days writing for a newspaper, much less the glory of the *Toronto Star*'s op-ed page. It happened for two good reasons, both of which I suggest are the essence of fine journalism. One is that he had something to say and the other is that he knew how to say it well. And it wasn't such a transformation at all for him to move from politician to journalist, because journalism stands at the heart of democracy. Politicians used to be ardent about democracy, though now it's rather rare and even electrifying to find a politician who cares more about principle than he or she does about being re-elected. Hello Tommy Douglas, we love you! Hello Bob Stanfield, we love you too! And hello Carolyn Bennett, you are classy! Journalists have an advantage over politicians because they can be indifferent to opinion polls. To be sure, they cut their cloth to fit other contours than their own, but the best journalists are inherently freelancers, a term first applied to those medieval knights who were not pledged to a lord. Their lances were their own. They were free of encumbrance and they could choose their battles. A part of the journalist's mandate, as I see it, is to rock the boat. This is done by seeing what is in the spaces between received wisdom and reality and by putting into public view hard-won information that authorities would prefer to hide. If journalists don't do that, who will? In the absence of accountability it is natural for people in power to behave badly. When the safety net begins to shred, as it has, when corruption or bad ideas invade legislature, as they do, a free press assuredly is the public's first line of defence. Journalists have changed the history of this country, and they've usually paid the price. The first on record were messieurs Bedard, Blanchet, and Taschereau who launched a newspaper in 1803 called *Le Canadien* with the motto Our Language, Our Institutions, Our Laws. Those distinct society pioneers speedily found themselves in prison where they were held without trial, which is the quintessential Canadian response to perceived troublemakers. We did it again in World War One when we put Ukrainians in internment camps and in World War Two when we imprisoned Italian-Canadians in Montreal and Japanese-Canadians in British Columbia. And it happened again with the War Measures Act in 1970 when five hundred French Canadians went to prison without charges being laid, and without the right to see a lawyer, and without the right to have bail. Early in the 1800s Halifax journalist Joseph Howe was hauled into court because his newspaper had complained about the dubious quality of justice in Nova Scotia. A few years after that William Lyon Mackenzie's presses were destroyed and thrown into Toronto harbour when he opposed the way a clique of powerful men ran Upper Canada. And Armor de Cosmo, an authentic West Coast eccentric who founded the *British Colonist* in Victoria in 1858 was a force for establishing responsible government in BC. A personal favourite of mine is Bob Edwards, who launched the *Eye Opener* in Alberta in 1902. He especially detested the Canadian Pacific Railway. His front page regularly featured pictures of CPR derailments and collisions. On off-days the headlines would read, "There are No CPR Wrecks This Week." And the cutlines under a picture of R.B. Bennett, then the CPR lawyer and later prime minister of Canada read "Another CPR Wreck!" When Alberta's first lieutenant governor arrived in Edmonton Bob Edwards noted that he was escorted by a bodyguard of influential real estate sharks. Raise a toast!

The significant factor in the ability of all these worthy men to brandish anti-establishment views was of course that they owned their own news-papers. A.J. Liebling famously said freedom of the press is guaranteed only to those who own one. The Family Compact did not have shares in Mackenzie's *Colonial Advocate* or else the history of Canada might have been very different.

These days it's difficult to see much air between media owners, ruling political parties, and corporate Canada. With party leadership candidates receiving millions upon millions of dollars from banks, corporations, and the like, and elections costing the parties even more millions, also provided by the same sources, our governments are increasingly beholden to vested interests. The dependency of politicians on large donations tends to shape the political agenda, however much politicians insist that they are pure of heart. Sadly, rich media barons have a natural affinity for others with wealth. The dispossessed — children, the homeless, the old, people with disabilities, those who've come here from hardscrabble countries — have no voice in the corridors of power. Unless the media pay attention to this pulverizing imbalance, the change in this country will continue to be for the worst as the quality of life for poor people falls off the nation's radar screen.

We have the weapon of the ballot; of course, we can vote the rascals out. Picking up clues about malfeasance and incompetence from the media we sometimes discover at election time that the mighty engine of collective indignation has quietly produced a critical mass that junks the incumbents, a manifestation of democracy called an upset. Unhappily, the new government often bears a startling resemblance to the old, since it was financed almost exactly by the same people who supported the previous one.

Some blame for these seamless transitions lies with the handful of people who dominate the media, all of them successful tycoons. The sympathies of media owners rarely lie with those Canadians who are stuck in the country's discard bin, and media owners usually are not keen about strengthening environmental controls, either. This is not to say that contemporary media owners do not have a social conscience, because some of them do. Owners usually keep their thumbs off editorial content. Their influence is more subtle. What happens is that ambitious editors and editorial writers, columnists and commentators run interference for them. Newsrooms know what the owner thinks about the Kyoto Accord, for instance, and what the owner never thinks about, say, quality affordable daycare. A healthy sense of self-preservation therefore guides the assignment choices that editors make and the story ideas journalists submit, to an extent far more pervasive than people know.

A beat journalist once said to me, "I can only get away with a few stories criticizing prison conditions. That perspective is just not popular upstairs." The thousands of challenging investigative stories not written, not aired are like the man who wasn't there in the children's nursery rhyme. They are not there today and they won't be there tomorrow either.

Some stories don't happen for reasons that have more to do with the bottom line than with pleasing owners. Investigative journalism means tying up researchers and reporters for a long time and probably paying expensive travel costs. Media outlets, like the rest of us, have tightening budgets to meet. Big city newspapers with relatively ample resources sometimes do themselves and the profession great honour by assigning a team of dedicated journalists to a difficult story. In recent days, the *Toronto Star* looked at racial profiling by the police. There seems to be an inordinate number of arrests and confinements of black men. The *Star* gave the reporters time to do the job properly.

Occasionally radio and television outlets do the same and when that happens we're all the winners. Independent outlets and small papers have a more difficult time finding resources for investigative journalism because their very existence is a struggle. I'm thinking of the *Kingston Whig-Standard*, which in the 1980s allowed two women reporters, Anne Kershaw and Mary Lasovitch, eight months during which the main preoccupation was to research and write about the tragic life of a loser, Marlene Moore, who slipped through the cracks of protection agencies and eventually killed herself in Kingston's infamous prison for women. And there's the *Norfolk Virginian-Pilot*, not a major newspaper by any means, which, a few years ago, decided to form a public life team, made up of reporters whose job it was "to lead the community to discover itself and act on what it has learned." Now that's responsible journalism at its finest.

What's come to be called responsible journalism all too frequently is responsible only to the status quo. This country depends more than it knows on the handful of men and women who toil away to uncover abuses of power and get their stories printed and aired because of the sheer weight of their unassailable research and good writing. What keeps many bad guys honest, or at least more careful, is the knowledge that an enterprising journalist may someday find them out.

First of all, however, an employer or publisher has to back that reporter. When the Mount Cashel disgrace of priests sexually abusing boys first came to the attention of Newfoundland journalists, the publisher of St. John's *Evening Telegram* killed the story. Not long after the news finally broke, *Content* magazine, alas long gone from the Canadian scene, published a very fine account by Kevin Fox, which detailed how that bad decision was made. Incidentally, the Michener Awards, named for a former governor general, are given every year to publishers and other chiefs in the media industry who don't fold in the clutch. The prizes are presented to news organizations, rather than individuals, in recognition of the reality that, while a crusading reporter gets and deserves much splash for uncovering venality, someone else is paying the bills.

As an aside, another branch of journalism has sprung into being, that of spin doctors who are hired at lucrative salaries, much higher than a working journalist could ever command. The full-time activity of these odd people is to fill the air with smoke and mirrors for the sole purpose of distracting the public from effective journalism that nips at the clay feet of the mighty. It's a very strange line of work. But idealism can be expensive in the field of journalism. Columnist-advocates and journalists with a sense of mission are always in danger of becoming self-unemployed. In this country, heads roll quite frequently when journalists annoy testy owners. If the journalist's mortgage isn't paid off, if the journalist is the sole source of a family's income, if the journalist's children are ready for university, those journalists are not in a good position to immolate themselves in the fires of righteousness.

It must be said that journalists in any democracy, and certainly our own, are extraordinarily privileged when compared to journalists in countries where criticism of the authorities will result in prison, torture, and death. When despots seek to dominate and plunder they first must silence the writers and they do. A monument is being built in New York to the memory of Daniel Pearl, a reporter for the *Wall Street Journal* who was gruesomely killed early this year by Muslim extremists in Pakistan. The goal of the monument, a colleague explained, is to inspire journalists with the idea that "a good journalist always questions everything and always goes beyond conventional wisdom."

Fundamentally, the profession of journalism enjoys its finest moments when it speaks against oppression and greed, but journalism does a glorious job of celebrating the triumphs of human spirit that elevate us all. Few stories play as fine with the public as those about someone behaving well in a crisis. Accounts of the human potential for selfless courage, for ingenuity, for stamina are soul food in these hungry times. Speaking for myself only, I find them extremely difficult to write because I have an inclination to freeze. When the story is very moving, the writer is imbued with a sense of sacred responsibility not to blow it and this can be an intimidating state of mind. I'm thinking how a *Time* magazine columnist, Roger Rosenblatt, twenty years ago was faced with a story about The Man in the Water. He was one of six survivors of a February plane crash in the frigid Potomac River. The six people were seen clinging to a piece of the plane's tail that was adrift among patches of ice. The man in the water, as he came to be known, helped each of the others into the rescue helicopter's flotation ring, one at a time, came back and back. He helped each person in until all were saved, but not the man in the water. When the helicopter came back for the sixth time he had succumbed to hypothermia and had vanished. And what to say about that gallant individual? Well, Rosenblatt got it right, all eight hundred words of it. The column ended with this: "The man in the water pitted himself against an implacable, impersonal enemy. He fought it with charity. He held it to a standoff. He was the best we can do."

Most stories, however, are mundane, at least on their surface. What the flotsam of today's news consists of mainly is a snapshot presented by a reporter turned hit and run. Drive-by stories are the working journalist's bread and butter. It's a breeze to cover a story about a truck on its side in the middle of the road. Yup, it's a truck all right. Definitely a truck, lying down, no question about it. Police on scene. Hmmm, good detail. What will take considerably more time, and much ingenuity, and accomplished research skills is an examination of all the factors that caused that truck to fall on its side. Journalists are rarely given the chance to track down experts who know if truck loading practices are safe, what role was played by road conditions or faulty highway construction, the state of truck maintenance and engineering, the fatigue and stress experienced by truck drivers. Instead, the journalist has time the next day only to check to make sure the two-paragraph item about a fallen over truck got in the paper or on the air and then must hurry on to the next assignment, which is about a pig farm which is poisoning well water. Yup, lots of pigs. Ha ha! Whole bunch of pigs. Stinky, too. And that story might have, at best, a two-day shelf life. The long look is the one that serves the public best.

Some years ago in New York City, late at night, a young woman, Kitty Genovese, was pursued down the street by an attacker who stabbed her over and over. For about twenty minutes she ran from him, screaming all the while, only to be struck again and again until she died. Reporters learned that her shrieks had disturbed the sleep of about fifty people in nearby apartments and none of them attempted to help her. That most-worthy newspaper, the *New York Times*, gave the story to a diligent reporter who interviewed every one of the fifty people. Their excuses varied but all were plausible and within the range of normal behaviour. Some said they'd done nothing because they assumed someone else had already called the police. Others said it sounded like a domestic dispute and they decided not to interfere, it wasn't their business and so on. When the *Times* story appeared it was a straightforward, uninflected account of all the excuses together with a mention of how many times Kitty Genovese was stabbed and how long she screamed before she died. Many readers experienced a seismic shift in attitude. Innocent bystanders no longer felt innocent, at all. Several wrote the paper to say they had promised themselves that they would never fail to intervene the next time they believed someone was in trouble. And the reporter got a Pulitzer Prize.

The public good was well served by that story. People who read it gained an insight into collective responsibility. Communities are held together at a fundamental level by their understanding of their mutual obligation. We look out for one another simply because we are all human, each of us no more so or no less so than everyone else on earth. We are in this predicament called life together. When someone falls it could easily be us on the ground. In order to ensure that we'll be helped when we need it we have no choice but to come to the assistance of the fallen, all the fallen.

Similarly, if you want your freedom of speech protected you're obliged to protect the freedom of speech of others, but especially those who say appalling things. This means you will find yourself occasionally in the company of revolting people because you are defending their right to express their revolting ideas — never mind. Oliver Wendell Holmes, the great American jurist, memorably observed it takes no effort to defend the freedom of speech with which you agree, but the real test of principles is to protect the freedom of speech you detest. That lovely man Voltaire said it this way: "Monsieur l'abbé, I detest what you write but I would give my life to make it possible for you to continue to write." Anyway, censorship is a singularly futile exercise. Look at Jesus Christ, for instance, or Socrates. The state killed both of them but their ideas could not be suppressed. Freedom of speech is not an absolute, as the Canadian Civil Liberties Association taught me in the twenty-four years I was vice-president. Twenty-four years vice-president and never got to be president. Dalton Camp was president so that was all right. People's right to a fair trial cannot be infringed upon, for example, and our libel laws are among the strictest in the world in order to address those occasions when irretrievable malicious damage is done to reputations. But when we seek to suppress the merely objectionable, putting vague criteria highly subject to misapplication into our criminal code, as we have, we imperil democracy itself.

No story exists without a dense surround of context. Consider this tragic headline: "Prisoner on parole rapes and kills innocent woman." The public was outraged such a monster had been let loose. Later, a follow-up was written by a painstaking reporter. It turned out the prisoner had been subjected to appalling abuse as a child and then shunted to many, many foster homes and in some of them was further abused. He went to school unprepared to learn. He emerged illiterate. He spent most of his life in prison where he received no treatment but a lot of solitary confinement and then he was discharged penniless. Without skills and under lax supervision he was a ticking bomb. He might have had a choice not to harm others but he didn't, so ultimately the blame for what happened, this terrible deed, falls on him, but society surely has some complicity in the tragedy of his destructive life. That's what I call connecting the dots.

When journalists look at cause as well as effect the whole country has a chance to advance to the point where fewer trucks topple over, for instance, or maybe Canadians will begin to believe that children deserve, as a matter of natural right, a safe start and good educations. Improvements in supports for very young children might just enable them to be stable and affectionate adults, and imagine a country where most of the adults are stable and affectionate. What would we do with the under-used prisons and drug treatment programs and mental hospitals? It's a worry I'll never live long enough to share. I'm really old. I'm somewhere between calcium supplements and dead. But I hope someday this country will need fewer jailers and therapists and shelters instead of every year needing more. When we achieve a substantial number of citizens who come to understand the problem and want it fixed and fixed properly, the country acquires the kind of soul growth which is vastly satisfying and makes us all relax. The media are the messengers, which is not what Marshall McLuhan said at all. Elected people pay close attention to the newspapers on their doorsteps, the news clips they see and hear. If we had a whack of Canadians who were outraged by our high level of homelessness, for instance, how long would we continue to tolerate it in this prosperous country? This is not a wild-eyed notion. This is precisely how change happens. This is how democracies came to the decision to eliminate public floggings.

Which brings us to bias. There are no hermetically sealed journalists. We are all porous as hell to the vagaries of the opinions of others, to our own pious prejudices, and to a full deck of unshakable, wooly-headed views. There are books we should have read but didn't. Warning sounds that found us deaf, flashpoints in our natures that shatter our ability to reason. The artist of deceptively simple writing, the *New Yorker*'s E.B. White, once observed that all writing is slanted. Journalists can't be perpendicular, he said, but they should attempt to be upright. The upright journalist is not without strong opinions. A reporter cannot look into a community's underside, meet the leaders and the beggars every working day, and not form conclusions about how things should be. Columnists can take to their soapboxes, but other content in the media is supposed to be impartial. The public rightly doesn't believe that for an instant.

Truth comes in as many disguises and has more silly hats than the Queen. Subjectivity trumps objectivity every time.

Most issues are multifaceted but let's stay with two in order to present this two-sided dispute that I'm imagining. The perfectly honourable writer searches for authorities for one side of the debate, a side the writer happens to favour and knows well. The reporter finds impressive material, resounding quotes, and irrefutable documentation. Further along in the account a sentence says "others disagree." What follows is the silliest, weakest analysis anyone has ever heard from people so obscure their mothers believe them dead. But if you define editorial balance by column inch, justice seems to have been served. A photograph of a politician looking goofy is always front-page stuff, particularly if the editorial pages support the opponent. What passes for balanced reporting is sometimes in the category between unintentional mischief and plain fraud.

Reporters in all the media are being urged, no, required, to avoid becoming entangled in a cause because their appearance of impartiality will be compromised. This is an edict that bears some examination. It's well within the scope of good editing to detect if a story is being fairly represented. Press councils, acting on complaints from the public, measure the equity of reporting all the time. Conflict of interest rules properly concern themselves with reporters accepting gifts or paying sources but the interests being served when journalists are required to distance themselves from the underbelly of poverty, and despair, and pollution in this country is the interest of the elite. The first casualty of imposed isolation isn't truth, it's understanding. You'll notice that owners don't feel they have to be political eunuchs in order to demonstrate their probity. Is it possible that they think reporters are lesser beings than they are? No.

Robert Fulford got an award one time. It's one of several lifetime achievements he received in his long and meritorious career. This one was presented, I think, by the Canadian Journalism Foundation. In his acceptance speech he said his experience in journalism had taught him this: the self must be developed in freedom and independence but must be fulfilled through community. There's nothing amiss in a reporter having a good heart. Journalists have a front row seat in the public arena and they know, better than most, what's going on. If they're not allowed the participatory rights of other citizens it's the community's loss. That splendid investigative journalist Stevie Cameron started one of this country's earliest and best out of the cold programs for homeless and hungry people and I rest my case.

John Hersey went to Hiroshima soon after the world's first atomic bomb killed about a hundred thousand people in one second. He wrote in the *New Yorker* a story full of sympathy and horror that immeasurably influenced the world to abandon testing and to restrain the use of nuclear weapons. John Hersey said this about his profession: "A journalist in any effort to render truth has three responsibilities. To the reader, to his or her conscience and to the human subjects." I don't disagree with any of John Hersey's points but I suggest a deeper responsibility.

My view is that journalists also have an obligation to set themselves a high ethical standard and to be passionately driven to meet that goal. If you never find a taskmaster harder on you than you yourself are, you've got it right. This is the part of journalism no one sees. If you knock on one door and get a useful quote that's good luck. If you knock on twenty doors and finally get one useful quote that's good work but nobody knows except you. For example, you're researching a complicated piece and someone tells you they read a very helpful article about the subject about a year ago in a medical journal. That kind of tip happens all the time and it drives me crazy. Do you try to track it down? Who would know if you didn't? It's very tempting to forget about it. Like the fox who didn't get the grapes you can tell yourself the article would probably turn out to be sour anyway, totally irrelevant and outdated. It's your call whether to check it out or not and you make the decision in the cold solitude where you and your conscience dwell. Will you go after the article? In a word, yes.

Then there's the issue of accuracy. Accuracy is an obligation. It's not a fair weather frill. All stories have fixed verities — the names that must be spelled correctly, the quote must be exactly as it was said and not the much better way it should have been said. Sources who refuse to give their names are not tolerable without a lot of proof he or she really did exist. There's a very good writer I know who never arrives in a strange city without being driven to the assignment by a philosopher king whose profound views form the background of the story the journalist writes ten minutes later. The cab driver is of course a figment of the journalist's imminent deadline and his inability to find anyone real to quote except himself.

Maybe this contributes to the fact that readers don't believe much of what they read in magazines and newspapers. Ninety percent of libel cases decided by juries go against the press. But people are much less skeptical of radio and television and that's curious. Journalists who work outside print rarely display the worthy politician who can't think in sound bites or the inarticulate wrecks who form the majority of people living in shelters. Instead they find glib and camera-ready smoothies or, for a hard luck story, the college educated single mum temporarily down on her luck and freshly bathed. Advocacy groups put forward their finest specimens, of course, but as columnist Walter Goodman once said, the story gets prettified. Anna Quindlen sternly observed in a *New York Times* column nearly ten years ago you do not intentionally rearrange reality.

The vital aspect of the profession is the most visible piece and something I'm not sure that can be taught. It's quality writing. Fine writing is the donkeywork of journalism, never mind the tedium of research. A skill with words comes from many sources, among them quantities of reading, confidence in yourself, an ample store of knowledge, and a good ear. If you can't put the pieces of a story together with logical structure and some élan, all the effort that went into the preparation will have been for nothing because your story will wither, unread. When Timothy Findley was asked by aspiring writers how they could become authors he used to reply "Write, write, write." That's from a school of thought that advocates hours, years of practice in order to acquire any skill. Margaret Atwood embellishes his advice. She says, "Write, write, write and read, read, read!" I'm stunned when teachers in journalism schools tell me their students don't read newspapers and don't watch or listen to news programs. Would they turn out for the Montreal Canadiens without having learned how to skate? What in the world are they doing in journalism school apart from keeping their parents calm? My advice goes beyond Findley and Atwood, impressive as their suggestions are. I would add rewrite, rewrite, rewrite. Most of a rewrite consists of pruning back the peacock feathers. Anna Quindlen again, who left a column in the op-ed section of the *New York Times* to become a novelist, wrote recently of her view that journalism is a good training ground for novelists. She said, "I learned in newspapers to make every word count. All those years of being given 1,200 words, of having the 1,200 pared into 900 at 3 o'clock, of having to take out another 100 to shoehorn it in a hole in the layout: it teaches you to make the distinction between what is necessary and illuminating and what is simply you in love with the sound of your own voice."

Flat language flattens ideas. You've got to spin that research into gold or it won't shine. Get yourself a vocabulary because you'll need alert verbs and adjectives and if any of you ever begins an article with that lazy, pompous opening, "This is the story of" I will personally come wherever you are and strangle you. And if I am dead my ghost will come and sit on your head.

I have neglected to speak much about electronic journalism mostly because I don't know much about it. I don't even have my own website and also because I don't see much money in it as yet. As an investor and contributor to *Straight Goods*, which is an excellent example of good cybernetic muckraking, I'm in a position to know what a scramble it is to keep electronic journalism afloat. All I can say on the topic, therefore, is don't let publishers steal your electronic rights. If you're a freelancer, don't sign those contracts that require you to give up all rights of every kind in perpetuity. I kid you not, that's the language. That simply isn't fair. The courts are sporting this out but I firmly believe that electronic rights are not part of the package when a writer sells print rights. They're not publisher's freebies. Most freelancers are not in a good position to get uppity with publishers. I know that. That's why I'm part of a class action against the *Globe and Mail*. If we win, freelancers won't have to knuckle under and forgo income to which they are entitled. Change of subject.

You can be a good person without being a journalist. Lots of people do that. But you cannot be a good journalist without being a good person. You become a good person with practice, by doing good deeds. It's as simple as that. Bob Fulford once dug up a quote from Aristotle, "that to become a builder, you build. To become just, you perform just acts." Excellence is not an act but a habit and a good deed always matters, however small. Holding the door for a stranger behind is a contagious act. It spreads consideration for others and it eases tension. As Bernard Malamud once observed, any act of good is a diminution of evil in the world and therefore no kindness is insignificant. It will not be lost in the universe. Jean Cocteau said one time, "even if I do not understand what I am, it is what I must be. It is my only safeguard."

I'm so proud to be a journalist and I'm especially proud to be a woman journalist. If all other means of persuasion fail I can always cry. Guys can't do that, at least not yet. I relish the comradeship of journalism, the language we share that has no words, the respect that we sometimes get from a colleague for good work, which means more than praise from anyone else. Journalism provides one with a very interesting life. It's not a road to wealth but it has the potential to be fulfilling. You might consider fulfillment, as I do, a better reward than money. William Faulkner said writers should have on their tombstones, "He wrote the books and then he died." Looks good to me. I wouldn't mind. She was a journalist and then she died, satisfied.

October 23, 2002

JOE SCHLESINGER

The Fog of Journalism

In the fall of 2003, we called in from the field Canada's most senior foreign correspondent. Joe Schlesinger was nearing the end of a distinguished career covering the world for the CBC. He was a pure reporter who always turned away from opportunities to work a desk in order to stay on the story. A native of Vienna, he was raised in Czechoslovakia before being sent by his parents to England in 1939 as part of a rescue program for Jewish children. His parents were killed in the Holocaust. He had a long career in journalism before joining the CBC in the mid-1960s. On a cool October night we again overfilled our 140-seat theatre, setting up chairs in the wings on the stage as Schlesinger took us into the heart of the story that defined the correspondent's life — war.

It's an honour to be here, and also a challenge and a pleasure. It's an honour because Dalton Camp represents a benchmark of excellence and thoughtfulness in Canadian journalism, and a challenge because these lectures are dedicated to keeping alive the standards he set. It's also a pleasure because it gives me an opportunity — even forces me — to do something I haven't had the occasion to do for a long time: collect my thoughts on journalism.

It isn't that I never get to talk about journalism. Not at all. Most often, though, it's with colleagues, grousing — after one drink too many, perhaps — about editors who reduce pearls to pap, news organization bean counters who don't know beans about news, good reporters who can't write, and good writers who can't report, who have a hard time telling fact from fib.

Journalists are, of course, hardly alone in this. We all bitch and moan about our jobs and gossip about our colleagues. You could say it is part of any job description. Napoleon's most loyal soldiers did it in spades and the emperor fondly called them *les grognards*, the grumblers, a name they wore proudly. Well, we are all *grognards* at heart. Even — or maybe especially — when we love what we do.

But when it comes to the larger picture about our work, we are all too often neglectful. Whatever it is that we do, we are, for the most part, too immersed in doing it to reflect on why we do what we do, and where our work fits into the grander scheme of things. This forum, it seems to me, affords an all-too-rare chance to look up from what I've been doing most of my life to touch on these themes.

First, though, a caveat, a confession of bias. I first ventured into journalism at age fifteen, putting out a typed daily news bulletin for my schoolmates at a boarding school in deepest Wales. You could say then that I started my career as a war reporter. A war reporter of sorts, anyway.

I'll have you know that in 1944 I had, as far as I know, a worldwide scoop, even if it was a scoop only a handful of my schoolmates and teachers knew about. On the morning of June 6, after having listened to news reports on the BBC of air battles over France and naval activity in the English Channel, I wrote "the Second Front appears to have started." The Second Front, of course, was D-Day, the Allied invasion of France.

As my schoolmates came to breakfast and read the bulletin, they scoffed at what I had written. Their skepticism was, of course, justified. The information on which I based my conclusion was flimsy indeed. No responsible editor would have published it. Still, a couple of hours later the BBC broke into its programming with an announcement from Supreme Headquarters Allied Forces Europe that Allied troops had landed on the beaches of Normandy.

There are some who would say that six decades later I'm still prone to the same flights of fancy. I'd argue that I've learned a thing or two since then. But in one respect I have not changed. Sixty years after I took those first wobbly steps in journalism I'm still hopelessly stricken, even besotted, with the news bug. I can't imagine having done anything else. I feel privileged and grateful for having been able to spend my life watching and recording the world unfolding.

They say the universe is unfolding as it should. In my experience, though, our little corner of it, this world of ours, certainly has not. It was, in fact, the unholy turmoil and turbulence of my youth that turned me towards journalism. It wasn't that I couldn't leave the news alone; it was the news that would not leave me alone. Not when I was pecking out those news bulletins at school as a refugee from Nazi-occupied Czechoslovakia during World War Two, nor after the war, when the communists took over from the Nazis in my homeland and once again threatened everything that was dear and near to me.

I came to journalism then much as an alcoholic might turn to bar-keeping — to get close to a regular supply of what he needs most. In totalitarian societies run by malevolent regimes, news — true information as opposed to government propaganda — becomes a scarce and yet indispensable tool for survival. One day a thousand flowers may be allowed to bloom. The next, not a petal is left. To survive you need to know when and where the scythe will come swishing down next.

I mention all this because, when I was invited to give this lecture, it struck me that Dalton Camp and I had come to journalism from opposite directions. I, from a need to know; he, from a desire to share what he knew so well. Where he with his journalism taught, I passed on what I had just learned with a "gee, folks, take a look at what I've found; isn't that interesting?"

I admired Dalton because he didn't let his partisanship detract from his sense of moral direction. And he always seemed to know what he was talking about. He knew the country. He knew his beat. As for me knowing my beat, well, let's say that flitting from crisis to crisis and from country to country is very much flying on wings of wax, held aloft by a combination of terminal curiosity and chutzpah, hoping the heat of the conflict around you doesn't melt the wings and bring you crashing down.

The greatest difference, though, between what Dalton wrote about and the stories I covered was that his villains were just wrong-headed, incompetent, short-sighted, or perhaps greedy while mine were also frequently violent and even murderous. In his stories, the stakes were power, policies, and the public interest; in mine they were all too often life, limb, and liberty.

I hate to have to say this, but my life and career were shaped by violent events: by wars, revolution, persecution, and other disasters. As a kid I saw the Germans marching into Czechoslovakia and bombs falling from England's skies. As a journalist, I covered wars in Vietnam and in the rest of Indochina, war between India and Pakistan, guerrilla wars in Nicaragua and El Salvador, the insanely destructive civil war in Beirut as well as the Israeli invasion of Lebanon, the first intifada, the Soviet invasion of Afghanistan, and the first Gulf War.

You could say that I have seen more wars than many a professional soldier. Having said that, though, let me add quickly that I know next to nothing of military affairs. I wouldn't know how to lead a platoon to a church parade. And the only time I've fired a gun has been in target practice. But I do know a few things about soldiers in combat. And I certainly know quite a bit about the journalists who cover wars and the constant tug-of-war between the military and the media.

There is nothing new in this. Tensions between journalists and the people and institutions they cover are normal, whether it's in covering politics, business, or the local cop shop. The relationship wavers between being symbiotic and sharply adversarial.

Covering wars magnifies the dynamics of the relationship. First, there is the danger involved. "If one writes about war," Graham Greene wrote in *The Quiet American*, "self-respect demands that one occasionally shares the risks." That may sound a bit blasé, even supercilious. But it's true. Besides, there is nothing like being there and seeing it to help you understand what you're talking or writing about.

One of the greatest works of combat reportage is Francisco Goya's *The disasters of war*, a series of eighty-five etchings Goya did of the horrors of the guerrilla war in Spain against the troops of Napoleon. They all have pithy titles, such as *It serves you right* below a picture of a French soldier dying. Or, *One can't look* underneath an illustration of an execution. But for me, the most telling of his titles, below a depiction of the plight of fleeing civilians, is *Yo lo vi*. I saw it.

He saw it himself. And seeing the disasters of war changed him and his art, and gave his illustrations tremendous power. Goya, remember, was a court painter. Painting royalty and other powerful figures was the way he made his living. He was, you could say, "embedded" in the Spanish royal court. He painted whoever was in power, whether it was the Spanish royal family or Joseph Bonaparte, whom Napoleon installed on the Spanish throne. He did portraits of French generals as well as of their adversary, the Duke of Wellington.

But that didn't stop Goya from painting his subjects as he saw them. His portraits of Charles IV and his family display their ugliness and vulgarity. Ultimately, Goya paid a price for his forthrightness and floating loyalties; he was forced into exile and died there.

Perilous though life with the royals could be, war is different from life at court. The conventional techniques of eighteenth-century portraiture didn't suffice to describe the horrors of war. And so Goya adopted a new style, a dramatically brutal, almost impressionistic style that foreshadowed and influenced generations of late nineteenth-century painters. In a way, Goya also foreshadowed the work of modern war correspondents and photographers. Most of them also came to war from more pacific pursuits. They had covered politics, the courts, the cop shop, or Lions Club lunches before they came to witness the brutality of war.

Now, as many a political reporter will tell you, reporting on politics can also be a rough-and-tumble pursuit. But whether it's reporting on politicians or boxers going mano-a-mano, we don't participate; we keep score. The government versus the opposition, defence lawyers having a go at prosecutors, cops chasing robbers. We may get hit on the noggin if we stick our necks out and get into the line of fire. But normally we manage, are even obliged, to stay out of the fray.

In covering wars, revolutions, and other outbreaks of mass violence staying out of the fray is more difficult. You take cover, of course, when you can. And you can delude yourself for a while that you're not part of the conflict: that you are just an observer; that no one is really shooting at you; that the two sides are just shooting at each other.

But then comes the moment of truth. It came to me one fine day more than thirty years ago in a plane over Laos. It was a single-engine prop-driven two-seater antique from the Second World War. I was sitting behind the pilot as he dive-bombed North Vietnamese positions near Vientiane, then the royal capital of Laos. Suddenly, the plane rocked as a puff of anti-aircraft fire exploded to one side of us, then another, and another. There was nowhere to hide, no mistaking the fact that, by God, they were shooting at me. I was, as they say these days, well and truly embedded.

The same goes for being in just about any hot spot with a military unit. When the incoming fire is flying fast and furious, the more embedded you are, preferably in a trench or a bunker, the more troops and guns you have around you, the happier and safer you will feel. Those soldiers around you, for the time being at least, will be your very best friends. There's no better way to learn the basics of how wars are fought than operating with a small unit under intense fire.

How close reporters can get to the fighting depends to a large extent on the people who are doing the fighting. Soldiers, after all, do have some very persuasive means to discourage journalists from hanging around. Generally, if things are going well for their forces, generals welcome reporters to record their successes; if not, they'd rather keep them away.

I've experienced some of those swings from the Vietnam War to the first Gulf War. In Vietnam, for all the friction between journalists and U.S. forces, the U.S. command was in many ways exceedingly helpful. There was no censorship, and reporters had access to U.S. transportation. You could go to the Tan Son Nhut U.S. air base in Saigon and get a lift to just about anywhere in South Vietnam, to Hue or the Mekong Delta, to Dalat or Danang, and from there by chopper to wherever the action was. Not always, of course, but often enough.

For me, more than thirty years later, one of the memorable experiences of my life is flying in Huey helicopters, sitting at the open door. The whole world is at your feet. At the speed and height choppers travel, the earth below becomes a map alive. You can see the lay of the land, the shape of roofs, the twists of rivers and roads and the traffic on them. If the chopper dips low enough, the dots below became people, or at least the tops of the conical straw hats Vietnamese peasants wear, bullock carts, children splashing in a pond, and water buffalo wallowing in the mud.

But what you, of course, also saw in Vietnam were the ugly scars of war, destroyed villages and the huge craters left behind by bombs dropped from U.S. B-52s.

Choppers could not only get you there. Even better, they could also get you out, at times out of some tight spots. The ride I remember best was an almost-casual lift I got. My cameraman and I were standing in a clearing in the middle of nowhere, Lord knows where, trying to get out because it was about to get dark, and nights were dangerous in the Vietnamese countryside. We saw a helicopter, waved our arms, and the pilot came in closer to take a look. I signalled with my thumb to hitch a ride, and to my amazement the chopper actually came down and picked us up.

I don't think that would happen today. Seems to me that nowadays American pilots, in Iraq let's say, would be too suspicious of being drawn into a terrorist trap to take the risk. We, on the other hand, would have probably had to think twice before hailing a ride in case our signalling was misunderstood and got us nothing more than a burst of gunfire.

When the U.S. lost the Vietnam War, much of the U.S. government and certainly most of the military blamed the press, especially on TV coverage of the war. The willingness of the American public to continue the war, it seems to me, was undercut not by what journalists said on television or wrote in newspapers, but rather by a combination of the power of the TV images of the brutality, the tens of thousands of body bags coming home, and the draft of the sons of the middle class with its attendant revolt of the young.

The media were never forgiven. As the junior officers of the Vietnam War rose to be the generals in command of U.S. forces in other conflicts they set out to keep reporters as far away from the fighting as possible. And there's been friction ever since.

But then confrontations, even clashes between the military have been going on ever since journalists started covering wars, way back a century and a half ago with the arrival in the Crimea of William Howard Russell of the *Times* of London.

There are two salient things you should know about Russell. The first is that his epitaph in St. Paul's Cathedral in London states that he was "the first and greatest" war correspondent. The other is his own evaluation of his role in journalism as "the miserable parent of a luckless tribe." Russell was certainly right about the tribe. His progeny, up to the war correspondents of today, have gone through much of what he went through and have suffered from much of what ailed him.

In the Crimea of his day, as in places such as Iraq right now, friends were more troublesome than foes. Russell certainly got no help from the British army. During the Crimean War of 1854-56, British commanders sent him packing whenever he showed up in the field. They went to the extent of cutting down his tent when he did manage to pitch it within the army's lines.

In London, too, his critical reports won him detractors, among them some in the highest places. A former British secretary for war urged the army to lynch Russell. Queen Victoria was more than just not amused; she let it be known she was positively displeased with the *Times* and its star correspondent. Her consort, Prince Albert, called Russell "a miserable scribbler," an appellation we scribblers to this day consider an accolade.

With no co-operation from the army, Russell faced a situation all reporters, not just war correspondents, still face. And that is the fog of journalism, the fact that it is all too rare for us to be able to say, *yo lo vi,* "I saw it."

That so much of what we cover we have not seen ourselves; that we have to rely on what others say they saw; that the stories these witnesses tell often contradict each other; that we have to grope our way through layers of fog to find out what actually did happen; that the fog is all too often made harder to penetrate by smokescreens laid down by those trying to cover up what happened. Finally, there's our biggest adversary: time, the tyranny of deadlines that leaves a tangle of unresolved loose ends dangling from so many of our stories.

Where historians may spend a lifetime getting the story straight only to find the next generation telling them they got it wrong, we most often have only hours and sometimes even just minutes to let go of the story and get it out, messy wrinkles, awkward holes, crooked seams, and all.

Nowhere is that fog of journalism thicker and more impenetrable than on a battlefield. As one media maven put it, the fog of war makes for foggy news.

For Bill Russell, the hardest part was getting the soldiers who had taken part in the battles he had not witnessed to talk to him. The generals instructed junior officers not to give him any help. In the end, to his credit, Russell seemed always able to find someone who was willing to talk. When wars start going wrong there are usually soldiers eager to tell the tale, whether it's in the Crimea in the nineteenth century, Vietnam in the twentieth, or Iraq in the twenty-first.

But getting the tale second-hand has problems of its own, whether the story is about a war, the closed caucus meeting of the government party, a bank robbery, or just a plain old house fire. Get three witnesses to a fire and you could find yourself getting a story of three fires. Eyewitnesses frequently contradict each other, and synthesizing a coherent and accurate account out of their testimony can often be a challenge.

As I said before, there is no substitute for *yo lo vi*.

What made Russell famous was not just his coverage of the battles of the Crimean War but his accounts of what went on behind the scenes: the incompetence and arrogance of the aristocratic British officer class and the suffering of ordinary soldiers. His reports on the miserable care of wounded soldiers prompted Florence Nightingale to travel to the Crimea and lay the foundation of modern nursing. His dispatches on the disastrous conduct of the war by British commander-in-chief Lord Raglan and his officers led to the downfall of the British government.

Russell's most famous account was of the disastrous battle of Balaclava on October 25, 1854.

"At ten minutes past eleven," he wrote, "our Light Cavalry Brigade advanced. They swept proudly past, glittering in all the pride and splendour of war." He went on about the smoke, the flames, and the fog of battle and ended his dispatch with this: "At thirty-five minutes past eleven," that's twenty-five minutes after the battle had started, "not a British soldier, except the dead and the dying, was left in front of the Muscovite guns."

That, as we know, led to this by Alfred, Lord Tennyson:

"Forward the Light Brigade!"
Was there a man dismay'd?
Not tho' the soldiers knew
  Someone had blunder'd:
Their's not to make reply,
Their's not to reason why,
Their's but to do and die.

It's all there in that piece of poetry. The bravery, the butchery, the stupidity.

Lord Raglan's order to the commander of the Light Brigade, Lord Cardigan, was to advance rapidly to prevent the enemy "carrying away the guns." Raglan meant the British guns that he saw from his position on top of the hill, which were in danger of being carried away. Cardigan, in the valley below, could not see the British guns, which were to his right. He thought his orders referred to the Russian guns he saw straight ahead. And so the Light Brigade charged the Russian positions head-on.

It was a massacre caused by stupidity and the foppish dilettantism of the aristocrats who ran the British military establishment. Yet it was also a tale of heroism, of self-sacrifice, and devotion to duty and honour. Taking the dichotomy of these two aspects of the battle into account in telling the story posed a dilemma for Bill Russell, a dilemma that in war after war still bedevils combat correspondents.

Russell resolved it by confining his contempt for the generals to his diary. "I looked at the group of officers representing the military mind of England close at hand in this crisis," he wrote, "and I was not much impressed with confidence by what I saw."

To his paper, though, he filed a story of pride and splendour. "With a halo of steel above their heads," he wrote, "and with a cheer which was many a noble fellow's death cry, they flew into the smoke of the batteries."

In other words, Russell censored himself. And when he didn't, his editors in London did. Some of his more inflammatory articles never made it into the *Times*. The editor, though, did send them to friends in government, letting them know what a hash their generals were making of the war.

The point here is that Russell and the *Times* were hardly rabble-rousers. They were part of the establishment. And they were horrified by what was happening in the Crimea. Their dilemma was the question of which was more patriotic: exposing the senseless slaughter of British soldiers or supporting the war effort by keeping quiet. So they compromised. They raised the issues of the mismanagement of the war but kept many of the more egregious instances of it from their readers.

What's true of Russell and the *Times* is true of later journalists, too. It's one thing to expose the mighty. Journalists may even revel in it. But not in wartime, not when your countrymen are fighting and dying. Criticism, however well-founded, can be equated with something akin to treason.

That goes not just for the reporters, but for their bosses, too. It was certainly on the mind of John Delane, Bill Russell's boss, when he carefully chose which of his correspondent's correspondence to print and which to leak discreetly to members of the British cabinet. Many of today's American editors have had to make the same calculation in how far to go in risking the rage of potent rightist pressure groups and the disapproval of their audiences and society at large.

In the two world wars, journalists had no such problem. On both sides everyone but everyone stayed onside. There wasn't any choice.

In World War One, correspondents were simply kept away from the fighting. If they were allowed anywhere near the front it was under tight restrictions. There were a few scribblers, brave souls who defied the military. When caught, though, they were jailed and threatened with being put up against a wall and shot if they did it again.

All news of the war was censored, manipulated, distorted, falsified. The butchery of millions in the trenches was minimized. Atrocity stories were made up out of whole cloth. The German press ran stories about German soldiers having their eyes gouged out; the British and French about Germans bayoneting children and cutting off women's breasts.

And the journalists just went along with it. As Ernest Hemingway put it, "the writers either wrote propaganda, shut up or fought."

The British prime minister, David Lloyd George, felt he had no choice but to keep the horrendous losses secret. "If people really knew," he told the editor of the *Manchester Guardian*, "the war would be stopped tomorrow. But of course they don't know and can't know. The correspondents don't write and the censorship would not pass the truth."

To a somewhat less stringent degree much the same thing can be said of the Second World War. All war dispatches were censored. But so was all private mail. Correspondents wore uniforms. German journalists were simply conscripted into the army. As for British war correspondents, the big question was whether their insignia should be a C for correspondent or, as many army officers would have preferred, a more explicit WC.

In Canada, there was a Directorate of Censorship as well as a Wartime Information Board whose role was to boost morale. There was some fine reporting done in World War Two, much of it by Canadians such as Ross Munro, Gregory Clark, the CBC's Matthew Halton, and Peter Stursberg. But propaganda then was hardly a dirty word. Only the other side's propaganda.

Then came Vietnam, and everything changed. It changed because it was, at first, not an American war. Yes, there were American soldiers there, but merely as "advisers." While censorship might have worked in Vietnam itself, this could not prevent journalists from filing critical findings from outside the country. The rest of the world, the U.S. included, was after all not a war zone where censorship could be imposed.

As Bill Russell was in his day, the small group of mainly American journalists in Saigon who wrote critically about the war from its early stages—people the White House and the Pentagon regarded as trouble-makers—were torn about what they were doing.

David Halberstam, the *New York Times* reporter who won a Pulitzer Prize for his coverage of Vietnam, put it this way: "We would have liked nothing better than to believe that the war was going well, and that it would eventually be won. But it was impossible to believe these things without denying the evidence of our senses."

Washington countered the critical reporting coming out of Saigon by launching a professional public relations campaign. All through the late sixties when the U.S. had as many as half a million soldiers there, the Americans encouraged journalists to go to Vietnam — even flew some of them over — for show-and-tell tours to get across its own version of the war. Tellingly, JUSPAO, the U.S. public affairs office, which handled relations with the media in Saigon, was also charged with psychological warfare.

It didn't work. JUSPAO held daily briefings in Saigon on the progress of the war. At the "five o'clock follies," as they became known, briefers dispensed inflated enemy body counts and minimized American and South Vietnamese losses. Nothing new in that either, of course. But by making the Vietnam War accessible to so many journalists, they lost control. Too many of us had covered the actions the briefers were reporting on, and in too many cases what we heard at the "follies" did not square with what we had seen.

There was also another element. As opposed to other wars, such the one in Crimea, the two world wars, or even the Gulf War, there was no single frontline. The war in Vietnam was everywhere. You could turn around the next corner, and there was the war or some aspect of it. If you couldn't get to whatever action there was in the central highlands, a short trip to the Mekong Delta would undoubtedly yield another story.

Now, let's face it, most reporters knew little about military affairs. Besides, most of what they witnessed was small, isolated segments of the war, small unit firefights, not the big military picture. But there was a pattern that could not be ignored, evidence ranging from the low morale of U.S. troops, from drug addiction to the fragging, that is, the killing of officers, the corruption of the South Vietnamese regime and its officers, to the disillusionment of the civilian population.

They knew all that in Washington, too, of course, even if they didn't admit it. And they acted on it, negotiating an armistice with the communists and then abandoning South Vietnam to its fate even as they pretended to defend it.

The fall-out of Vietnam is still with us. At first, the Pentagon reacted by simply barring the media from its operations. During the U.S. invasion of Grenada in 1983, the Pentagon provided transport for some three hundred journalists. But instead of flying them to Grenada, they flew them to Barbados, 250 kilometres away from the fighting, where they spoon-fed them with accounts of the invasion. Reporters who tried to land by boat were turned away at gunpoint. Six years later, during the invasion of Panama, journalists were held over at airports in Miami and Costa Rica until the action was all over and it was considered safe to let them see the aftermath.

It wasn't just the Americans. During the Falklands War, Britain's Royal Marines took only a handful of reporters along to the war zone. No TV cameras were allowed, and all reports had to be filed over marine radio after being censored. News organizations protested, of course. But it didn't do them much good.

By the time the first Gulf War came along, the Pentagon realized it couldn't handle press relations in a large war waged by a coalition as it did during tight little operations such as Panama and Grenada. So it came up with a system of pool coverage, that is, taking along one or two reporters to represent the whole press corps and then making their material available to all. Now, pools are an everyday journalistic arrangement to avoid having a horde of journalists swamping an event.

But the way it was managed in Saudi Arabia in the press hotel in Dhahran, way behind the frontlines, was bit of a boondoggle. Most of the pool positions were given to large U.S. news organizations. Pool crews were accompanied by military escort officers who sat in on all interviews to make sure soldiers didn't say anything they didn't want said. It wasn't called censorship anymore; "security review" was the new term and it was often petty and cosmetic. For example, one reporter complained that when he described the mood of pilots returning from a successful mission as "giddy," the censors changed it to "proud."

The rest of the press corps — and that went for Canadian reporters in spades — was stuck watching this pool material coming in and gluing together some semblance of a story. In a way, you couldn't leave Dhahran because you might miss something significant coming out of the maw of the pool machine.

Besides, getting to the front on your own was mission impossible. Unlike Vietnam or El Salvador or Lebanon, where, if you got stopped at one roadblock you could always find a different road, there was only one highway from Dhahran north to Kuwait and the front. And off the road, nothing but desert. You needed not just a great deal of luck but also influence to stand a chance. It was one of the most frustrating assignments I'd ever had.

When the Allied ground offensive started, though, the system broke down. It worked as long as the frontline was static, as coalition forces used their air superiority and artillery to soften up the Iraqis. Once the Allied armies were on the move, it was relatively easy to slip past roadblocks by melding our vehicle, unnoticed, into the middle of a military convoy. We managed to wend our way into Kuwait between the U.S. and Saudi forces to do what we were meant to do: report first-hand on what was going on.

Yo lo vi.

Fast forward to next Gulf War, and you have a new wrinkle in trying to control the media in war. And that is the "embedding" of journalists.

It means assigning journalists to individual units to accompany them more or less for the duration.

While embedding gives reporters and camera people closer access to combat unit operations, it has several disadvantages. The first is that if a news organization had, let's say, two reporters in Iraq, it could not afford to leave one of them isolated with just one unit; it would need the flexibility to have them both cover various aspects of the war, in Baghdad, Basra, at coalition headquarters, or wherever.

Besides, what you got depended on the unit to which you were assigned. If you were Canadian that wasn't much. Among the assignments offered to Canadian news organizations was a spot with a U.S. air defence battery in Kuwait. Given that the Iraqi air force never got off the ground, that assignment would have amounted to ending up with thumbs sore from endless twiddling. You couldn't just pack up and transfer to some outfit that was more involved in the fighting.

Not signing on, on the other hand, as an "embed," as they call them, left journalists in a difficult position. Dubbed by the Pentagon as "unilaterals," they were denied access to U.S. forces, harried at roadblocks, and in general treated by the Americans as pariahs.

Being embedded carried with it its own problems. For one, there was a list of ground rules. Most of them were reasonable enough: not reporting on the location of the unit you were attached to, or the number of troops or equipment. I don't think any journalist would want to endanger the lives of the troops he or she were with.

In the end, how much access embeds got to action depended on how the commanders of the units they were with interpreted the rules, whether they believed that what a journalist had reported or might report endangered their operations. It was the commanders' call, apparently a call that, at times, was made quite arbitrarily.

Much has been made of the perception that embeds could not do their jobs properly because they were captives of the military, that this would taint them as tools of U.S. propaganda, that the military might even feed them, horror of horrors, false information.

Lordy, lordy, lord. Fancy that now. No other organization, of course, would ever think of pulling the wool over the eyes of journalists. Not the nice spin doctors in other branches of the government, nor the armies of flacks of various companies and other institutions.

What bothers me about the embed phenomenon is not the embedding itself; it was what happened to those who were not embedded, the downright nastiness of the Pentagon's handling of the media that were not, so to speak, "on the team." The extension of the Bush administration's predilection of seeing the world in terms of "if you're not with us, you're against us."

I wasn't there. But it must have been frustrating, and I must give all credit to the unilaterals, including my colleagues at the CBC TV News — Patrick Brown, Don Murray, Paul Workman, and their crews — for the great work they did under difficult and dangerous conditions.

For journalists, it was certainly a dangerous war. A dozen media workers were killed, five of them by friendly fire. Some were embeds, some unilaterals, and others lost their lives while working in Baghdad when it was still in Saddam Hussein's hands. It was proportionately a much higher casualty rate than that of the U.S. and British military.

Still, for journalists the most dangerous wars are not conflicts between armies. They are civil and guerrilla wars in which there is often no frontline, no central command, little discipline, and a lot of hate.

The most dangerous of these wars was probably the conflict in Bosnia. Sixty-two journalists, most of them local, were killed as Serbs, Croats, and Muslims fought not just each other but, as it sometimes seemed, the whole world. This is the kind of war the world is seeing more of, small wars driven by an "us against the world" mentality. Such is the hate that no one is safe, least of all civilians, whether they are innocent bystanders or journalists.

It is not a good time to be a war correspondent.

In a way, it reminds me of one of the lighter moments of the war in El Salvador, where in the eighties the press corps faced not just the dangers of the fighting between government forces and the guerrillas but also death threats from the ultra-rightist death squads. In a fit of gallows humour, some wag had a bunch of T-shirts made. One side had a big bull's eye and on the other the inscription "no tirar, periodista" — don't shoot, journalist.

Needless to say the shirts were a sell-out. They reminded us that it made no difference which side we wore on the front and which on the back. Que sera, sera.

As I said, I wasn't there in the second Gulf War, having realized in the first one that I was older than anyone around, older by a decade than even the generals. It was time to pack it in.

Luckily, I had done more than just cover wars, and, thank heavens, there is a lot more going on in this world than wars. Interesting and important things. Enough of them to keep me busy working, constantly learning, I hope, for a long time. Learning and seeing it with your own eyes is what makes journalism such a joy.

Yo lo vi y lo dije.

I saw it and told it.

I am, and always shall be, grateful for having had the privilege of doing it.

October 30, 2003

NAOMI KLEIN
Baghdad Year Zero

When we invited journalist and activist Naomi Klein to campus in the fall of 2004, five years after the international success of her bestselling first book, No Logo: Taking Aim at the Brand Bullies, *she was a literary star. She had recently returned from a trip to Iraq for* Harper's Magazine, *which would form the foundation of her next book,* Shock Doctrine: The Rise of Disaster Capitalism. *We expected she would draw a crowd, so we moved the lecture into the four-hundred-seat St. Thomas University chapel and set up an overflow room downstairs in the cafeteria. When Klein arrived and discovered the overflow room was full, she insisted on stopping there first to address them in person for a few minutes. She said she is always running late; the people in the overflow room were her people. A version of the talk she gave that evening was published in* Harper's.

It was only after I had been in Baghdad for a month that I found what I was looking for. I had travelled to Iraq a year after the war began, at the height of what should have been a construction boom, but after weeks of searching I had not seen a single piece of heavy machinery apart from tanks and Humvees. Then I saw it: a construction crane. It was big and yellow and impressive, and when I caught a glimpse of it around a corner in a busy shopping district I thought that I was finally about to witness some of the reconstruction I had heard so much about. But as I got closer I noticed that the crane was not actually rebuilding anything — not one of the bombed-out government buildings that still lay in rubble all over the city, nor one of the many power lines that remained in twisted heaps even as the heat of summer was starting to bear down. No, the crane was hoisting a giant billboard to the top of a three-storey building: SUNBULA: HONEY 100% NATURAL, made in Saudi Arabia.

Seeing the sign, I couldn't help but think about something Senator John McCain had said back in October. Iraq, he said, is "a huge pot of honey that's attracting a lot of flies." The flies McCain was referring to were the Halliburtons and Bechtels, as well as the venture capitalists who flocked to Iraq in the path cleared by Bradley Fighting Vehicles and laser-guided bombs. The honey that drew them was not just no-bid contracts and Iraq's famed oil wealth but the myriad investment opportunities offered by a country that had just been cracked wide open after decades of being sealed off, first by the nationalist economic policies of Saddam Hussein, then by asphyxiating United Nations sanctions.

Looking at the honey billboard, I was also reminded of the most common explanation for what has gone wrong in Iraq, a complaint echoed by everyone from John Kerry to Pat Buchanan: Iraq is mired in blood and deprivation because George W. Bush didn't have "a postwar plan." The only problem with this theory is that it isn't true. The Bush administration did have a plan for what it would do after the war; put simply, it was to lay out as much honey as possible, then sit back and wait for the flies.

The honey theory of Iraqi reconstruction stems from the most cherished belief of the war's ideological architects: that greed is good. Not good just for them and their friends but good for humanity, and certainly good for Iraqis. Greed creates profit, which creates growth, which creates jobs and products and services and everything else anyone could possibly need or want. The role of good government, then, is to create the optimal conditions for corporations to pursue their bottomless greed, so that they in turn can meet the needs of the society. The problem is that governments, even neoconservative governments, rarely get the chance to prove their sacred theory right: despite their enormous ideological advances, even George Bush's Republicans are, in their own minds, perennially sabotaged by meddling Democrats, intractable unions, and alarmist environmentalists.

Iraq was going to change all that. In one place on earth, the theory would finally be put into practice in its most perfect and uncompromised form. A country of twenty-five million would not be rebuilt as it was before the war; it would be erased, disappeared. In its place would spring forth a gleaming showroom for laissez-faire economics, a utopia such as the world had never seen. Every policy that liberates multinational corporations to pursue their quest for profit would be put into place: a shrunken state, a flexible workforce, open borders, minimal taxes, no tariffs, no ownership restrictions. The people of Iraq would, of course, have to endure some short-term pain: assets, previously owned by the state, would have to be given up to create new opportunities for growth and investment. Jobs would have to be lost and, as foreign products flooded across the border, local businesses and family farms would, unfortunately, be unable to compete. But to the authors of this plan, these would be small prices to pay for the economic boom that would surely explode once the proper conditions were in place, a boom so powerful the country would practically rebuild itself.

The fact that the boom never came and Iraq continues to tremble under explosions of a very different sort should never be blamed on the absence of a plan. Rather, the blame rests with the plan itself, and the extraordinarily violent ideology upon which it is based.

Torturers believe that when electrical shocks are applied to various parts of the body simultaneously subjects are rendered so confused about where the pain is coming from that they become incapable of resistance. A declassified CIA counterintelligence interrogation manual from 1963 describes how a trauma inflicted on prisoners opens up "an interval—which may be extremely brief—of suspended animation, a kind of psychological shock or paralysis.... At this moment the source is far more open to suggestion, far likelier to comply." A similar theory applies to economic shock therapy, or "shock treatment," the ugly term used to describe the rapid implementation of free-market reforms imposed on Chile in the wake of General Augusto Pinochet's coup. The theory is that if painful economic "adjustments" are brought in rapidly and in the aftermath of a seismic social disruption like a war, a coup, or a government collapse, the population will be so stunned, and so preoccupied with the daily pressures of survival, that it too will go into suspended animation, unable to resist. As Pinochet's finance minister, Admiral Lorenzo Gotuzzo, declared, "The dog's tail must be cut off in one chop."

That, in essence, was the working thesis in Iraq, and in keeping with the belief that private companies are more suited than governments for virtually every task, the White House decided to privatize the task of privatizing Iraq's state-dominated economy. Two months before the war began, USAID began drafting a work order, to be handed out to a private company, to oversee Iraq's "transition to a sustainable market-driven economic system." The document states that the winning company (which turned out to be the KPMG offshoot BearingPoint) will take "appropriate advantage of the unique opportunity for rapid progress in this area presented by the current configuration of political circumstances." Which is precisely what happened. L. Paul Bremer, who led the U.S. occupation of Iraq from May 2, 2003, until he caught an early flight out of Baghdad on June 28, admits that when he arrived, "Baghdad was on fire, literally, as I drove in from the airport." But before the fires from the "shock and awe" military onslaught were even extinguished, Bremer unleashed his shock therapy, pushing through more wrenching changes in one sweltering summer than the International Monetary Fund has managed to enact over three decades in Latin America. Joseph Stiglitz, Nobel laureate and former chief economist at the World Bank, describes Bremer's reforms as "an even more radical form of shock therapy than pursued in the former Soviet world."

The tone of Bremer's tenure was set with his first major act on the job: he fired 500,000 state workers, most of them soldiers, but also doctors, nurses, teachers, publishers, and printers. Next, he flung open the country's borders to absolutely unrestricted imports: no tariffs, no duties, no inspections, no taxes. Iraq, Bremer declared two weeks after he arrived, was "open for business."

One month later, Bremer unveiled the centrepiece of his reforms. Before the invasion, Iraq's non-oil-related economy had been dominated by two hundred state-owned companies, which produced everything from cement to paper to washing machines. In June, Bremer flew to an economic summit in Jordan and announced that these firms would be privatized immediately. "Getting inefficient state enterprises into private hands," he said, "is essential for Iraq's economic recovery." It would be the largest state liquidation sale since the collapse of the Soviet Union.

But Bremer's economic engineering had only just begun. In September, to entice foreign investors to come to Iraq, he enacted a radical set of laws unprecedented in their generosity to multinational corporations. There was Order 37, which lowered Iraq's corporate tax rate from roughly forty percent to a flat fifteen percent. There was Order 39, which allowed foreign companies to own one hundred percent of Iraqi assets outside of the natural-resource sector. Even better, investors could take one hundred percent of the profits they made in Iraq out of the country; they would not be required to reinvest and they would not be taxed. Under Order 39, they could sign leases and contracts that would last for forty years. Order 40 welcomed foreign banks to Iraq under the same favourable terms. All that remained of Saddam Hussein's economic policies was a law restricting trade unions and collective bargaining.

If these policies sound familiar, it's because they are the same ones multinationals around the world lobby for from national governments and in international trade agreements. But while these reforms are only ever enacted in part, or in fits and starts, Bremer delivered them all, all at once. Overnight, Iraq went from being the most isolated country in the world to being, on paper, its widest-open market.

At first, the shock-therapy theory seemed to hold: Iraqis, reeling from violence both military and economic, were far too busy staying alive to mount a political response to Bremer's campaign. Worrying about the privatization of the sewage system was an unimaginable luxury with half the population lacking access to clean drinking water; the debate over the flat tax would have to wait until the lights were back on. Even in the international press, Bremer's new laws, though radical, were easily upstaged by more dramatic news of political chaos and rising crime.

Some people were paying attention, of course. That autumn was awash in "rebuilding Iraq" trade shows, in Washington, London, Madrid, and Amman. *The Economist* described Iraq under Bremer as "a capitalist dream," and a flurry of new consulting firms were launched promising to help companies get access to the Iraqi market, their boards of directors stacked with well-connected Republicans. The most prominent was New Bridge Strategies, started by Joe Allbaugh, former Bush-Cheney campaign manager. "Getting the rights to distribute Procter & Gamble products can be a gold mine," one of the company's partners enthused. "One well-stocked 7-Eleven could knock out thirty Iraqi stores; a Wal-Mart could take over the country."

Soon there were rumours that a McDonald's would be opening up in downtown Baghdad, funding was almost in place for a Starwood luxury hotel, and General Motors was planning to build an auto plant. On the financial side, HSBC would have branches all over the country, Citigroup was preparing to offer substantial loans guaranteed against future sales of Iraqi oil, and the bell was going to ring on a New York–style stock exchange in Baghdad any day.

In only a few months, the postwar plan to turn Iraq into a laboratory for the neocons had been realized. Leo Strauss may have provided the intellectual framework for invading Iraq pre-emptively, but it was that other University of Chicago professor, Milton Friedman, author of the anti-government manifesto *Capitalism and Freedom*, who supplied the manual for what to do once the country was safely in America's hands. This represented an enormous victory for the most ideological wing of the Bush administration. But it was also something more: the culmination of two interlinked power struggles, one among Iraqi exiles advising the White House on its postwar strategy, the other within the White House itself.

As the British historian Dilip Hiro has shown, in *Secrets and Lies: Operation "Iraqi Freedom" and After*, the Iraqi exiles pushing for the invasion were divided, broadly, into two camps. On one side were "the pragmatists," who favoured getting rid of Saddam and his immediate entourage, securing access to oil, and slowly introducing free-market reforms. Many of these exiles were part of the State Department's Future of Iraq Project, which generated a thirteen-volume report on how to restore basic services and transition to democracy after the war. On the other side was the "Year Zero" camp, those who believed that Iraq was so contaminated that it needed to be rubbed out and remade from scratch. The prime advocate of the pragmatic approach was Iyad Allawi, a former high-level Baathist who fell out with Saddam and started working for the CIA. The prime advocate of the Year Zero approach was Ahmad Chalabi, whose hatred of the Iraqi state for expropriating his family's assets during the 1958 revolution ran so deep he longed to see the entire country burned to the ground — everything, that is, but the oil ministry, which would be the nucleus of the new Iraq, the cluster of cells from which an entire nation would grow. He called this process "de-Baathification."

A parallel battle between pragmatists and true believers was being waged within the Bush administration. The pragmatists were men like Secretary of State Colin Powell and General Jay Garner, the first U.S. envoy to postwar Iraq. General Garner's plan was straightforward enough: fix the infrastructure, hold quick and dirty elections, leave the shock therapy to the International Monetary Fund, and concentrate on securing U.S. military bases on the model of the Philippines. "I think we should look right now at Iraq as our coaling station in the Middle East," he told the BBC. He also paraphrased T.E. Lawrence, saying, "It's better for them to do it imperfectly than for us to do it for them perfectly." On the other side was the usual cast of neoconservatives: Vice-President Dick Cheney, Secretary of Defense Donald Rumsfeld (who lauded Bremer's "sweeping reforms" as "some of the most enlightened and inviting tax and investment laws in the free world"), Deputy Secretary of Defense Paul Wolfowitz, and perhaps most centrally, Undersecretary of Defense Douglas Feith. Whereas the State Department had its Future of Iraq report, the neocons had USAID's contract with BearingPoint to remake Iraq's economy: in 108 pages, privatization was mentioned no fewer than fifty-one times. To the true believers in the White House, General Garner's plans for postwar Iraq seemed hopelessly unambitious. Why settle for a mere coaling station when you can have a model free market? Why settle for the Philippines when you can have a beacon unto the world?

The Iraqi Year Zeroists made natural allies for the White House neoconservatives: Chalabi's seething hatred of the Baathist state fit nicely with the neocons' hatred of the state in general, and the two agendas effortlessly merged. Together, they came to imagine the invasion of Iraq as a kind of Rapture: where the rest of the world saw death, they saw birth — a country redeemed through violence, cleansed by fire. Iraq wasn't being destroyed by cruise missiles, cluster bombs, chaos, and looting; it was being born again. April 9, 2003, the day Baghdad fell, was day one of Year Zero.

While the war was being waged, it still wasn't clear whether the pragmatists or the Year Zeroists would be handed control over occupied Iraq. But the speed with which the nation was conquered dramatically increased the neocons' political capital, since they had been predicting a "cakewalk" all along. Eight days after George Bush landed on that aircraft carrier under a banner that said MISSION ACCOMPLISHED, the president publicly signed on to the neocons' vision for Iraq to become a model corporate state that would open up the entire region. On May 9, Bush proposed the "establishment of a U.S. - Middle East free trade area within a decade"; three days later, Bush sent Paul Bremer to Baghdad to replace Jay Garner, who had been on the job for only three weeks. The message was unequivocal: the pragmatists had lost; Iraq would belong to the believers.

A Reagan-era diplomat-turned-entrepreneur, Bremer had recently proven his ability to transform rubble into gold by waiting exactly one month after the September 11 attacks to launch Crisis Consulting Practice, a security company selling "terrorism risk insurance" to multinationals. Bremer had two lieutenants on the economic front: Thomas Foley and Michael Fleischer, the heads of "private sector development" for the Coalition Provisional Authority (CPA). Foley is a Greenwich, Connecticut, multimillionaire, a long-time friend of the Bush family, and a Bush-Cheney campaign "pioneer" who has described Iraq as a modern California "gold rush." Fleischer, a venture capitalist, is the brother of former White House spokesman Ari Fleischer. Neither man had any high-level diplomatic experience and both use the term corporate "turnaround" specialist to describe what they do. According to Foley, this uniquely qualified them to manage Iraq's economy because it was "the mother of all turnarounds."

Many of the other CPA postings were equally ideological. The Green Zone, the city within a city that houses the occupation headquarters in Saddam's former palace, was filled with Young Republicans straight out of the Heritage Foundation, all of them given responsibility they could never have dreamed of receiving at home. Jay Hallen, a twenty four year old who had applied for a job at the White House, was put in charge of launching Baghdad's new stock exchange. Scott Erwin, a twenty-one-year-old former intern to Dick Cheney, reported in an email home that "I am assisting Iraqis in the management of finances and budgeting for the domestic security forces." The college senior's favourite job before this one? "My time as an ice-cream truck driver." In those early days, the Green Zone felt a bit like the Peace Corps, for people who think the Peace Corps is a communist plot. It was a chance to sleep on cots, wear army boots, and cry "incoming" — all while being guarded around-the-clock by real soldiers.

The teams of KPMG accountants, investment bankers, think-tank lifers, and Young Republicans that populate the Green Zone have much in common with the IMF missions that rearrange the economies of developing countries from the presidential suites of Sheraton hotels the world over. Except for one rather significant difference: in Iraq they were not negotiating with the government to accept their "structural adjustments" in exchange for a loan; they were the government.

Some small steps were taken, however, to bring Iraq's U.S.-appointed politicians inside. Yegor Gaidar, the mastermind of Russia's mid-nineties privatization auction that gave away the country's assets to the reigning oligarchs, was invited to share his wisdom at a conference in Baghdad. Marek Belka, who as finance minister oversaw the same process in Poland, was brought in as well. The Iraqis who proved most gifted at mouthing the neocon lines were selected to act as what USAID calls local "policy champions" — men like Ahmad al Mukhtar, who told me of his countrymen, "They are lazy. The Iraqis by nature, they are very dependent.... They will have to depend on themselves, it is the only way to survive in the world today." Although he has no economics background and his last job was reading the English-language news on television, al Mukhtar was appointed director of foreign relations in the Ministry of Trade and is leading the charge for Iraq to join the World Trade Organization.

I had been following the economic front of the war for almost a year before I decided to go to Iraq. I attended the "Rebuilding Iraq" trade shows, studied Bremer's tax and investment laws, met with contractors at their home offices in the United States, interviewed the government officials in Washington who are making the policies. But as I prepared to travel to Iraq in March to see this experiment in free-market utopianism up close, it was becoming increasingly clear that all was not going according to plan. Bremer had been working on the theory that if you build a corporate utopia the corporations will come — but where were they? American multinationals were happy to accept U.S. taxpayer dollars to reconstruct the phone or electricity systems, but they weren't sinking their own money into Iraq. There was, as yet, no McDonald's or Wal-Mart in Baghdad, and even the sales of state factories, announced so confidently nine months earlier, had not materialized.

Some of the holdup had to do with the physical risks of doing business in Iraq. But there were other more significant risks as well. When Paul Bremer shredded Iraq's Baathist constitution and replaced it with what *The Economist* greeted approvingly as "the wish list of foreign investors," there was one small detail he failed to mention: it was all completely illegal. The CPA derived its legal authority from United Nations Security Council Resolution 1483, passed in May 2003, which recognized the United States and Britain as Iraq's legitimate occupiers. It was this resolution that empowered Bremer to unilaterally make laws in Iraq. But the resolution also stated that the U.S. and Britain must "comply fully with their obligations under international law including in particular the Geneva Conventions of 1949 and the Hague Regulations of 1907." Both conventions were born as an attempt to curtail the unfortunate historical tendency among occupying powers to rewrite the rules so that they can economically strip the nations they control. With this in mind, the conventions stipulate that an occupier must abide by a country's existing laws unless "absolutely prevented" from doing so. They also state that an occupier does not own the "public buildings, real estate, forests and agricultural assets" of the country it is occupying but is rather their "administrator" and custodian, keeping them secure until sovereignty is re-established. This was the true threat to the Year Zero plan: since America didn't own Iraq's assets, it could not legally sell them, which meant that after the occupation ended, an Iraqi government could come to power and decide that it wanted to keep the state companies in public hands or, as is the norm in the Gulf region, to bar foreign firms from owning one hundred percent of national assets. If that happened, investments made under Bremer's rules could be expropriated, leaving firms with no recourse because their investments had violated international law from the outset.

By November, trade lawyers started to advise their corporate clients not to go into Iraq just yet, that it would be better to wait until after the transition. Insurance companies were so spooked that not a single one of the big firms would insure investors for "political risk," that high-stakes area of insurance law that protects companies against foreign governments turning nationalist or socialist and expropriating their investments.

Even the U.S.-appointed Iraqi politicians, up to now so obedient, were getting nervous about their own political futures if they went along with the privatization plans. Communications Minister Haider al-Abadi told me about his first meeting with Bremer. "I said, 'Look, we don't have the mandate to sell any of this. Privatization is a big thing. We have to wait until there is an Iraqi government.'" Minister of Industry Mohamad Tofiq was even more direct: "I am not going to do something that is not legal, so that's it."

Both al-Abadi and Tofiq told me about a meeting — never reported in the press — that took place in late October 2003. At that gathering the twenty-five members of Iraq's governing council as well as the twenty-five interim ministers decided unanimously that they would not participate in the privatization of Iraq's state-owned companies or of its publicly owned infrastructure.

But Bremer didn't give up. International law prohibits occupiers from selling state assets themselves, but it doesn't say anything about the puppet governments they appoint. Originally, Bremer had pledged to hand over power to a directly elected Iraqi government, but in early November he went to Washington for a private meeting with President Bush and came back with a Plan B. On June 30 the occupation would officially end — but not really. It would be replaced by an appointed government, chosen by Washington. This government would not be bound by the international laws preventing occupiers from selling off state assets, but it would be bound by an "interim constitution," a document that would protect Bremer's investment and privatization laws.

The plan was risky. Bremer's June 30 deadline was awfully close, and it was chosen for a less-than-ideal reason: so that President Bush could trumpet the end of Iraq's occupation on the campaign trail. If everything went according to plan, Bremer would succeed in forcing a "sovereign" Iraqi government to carry out his illegal reforms. But if something went wrong, he would have to go ahead with the June 30 handover anyway because by then Karl Rove, and not Dick Cheney or Donald Rumsfeld, would be calling the shots. And if it came down to a choice between ideology in Iraq and the electability of George W. Bush, everyone knew which would win.

At first, Plan B seemed to be right on track. Bremer persuaded the Iraqi Governing Council to agree to everything: the new timetable, the interim government, and the interim constitution. He even managed to slip into the constitution a completely overlooked clause, Article 26. It stated that for the duration of the interim government, "The laws, regulations, orders and directives issued by the Coalition Provisional Authority... shall remain in force" and could only be changed after general elections are held.

Bremer had found this legal loophole: There would be a window — seven months — when the occupation was officially over but before general elections were scheduled to take place. Within this window, the Hague and Geneva Conventions' bans on privatization would no longer apply, but Bremer's own laws, thanks to Article 26, would stand. During these seven months, foreign investors could come to Iraq and sign forty-year contracts to buy up Iraqi assets. If a future elected Iraqi government decided to change the rules, investors could sue for compensation.

But Bremer had a formidable opponent: Grand Ayatollah Ali al Sistani, the most senior Shia cleric in Iraq. Al Sistani tried to block Bremer's plan at every turn, calling for immediate direct elections and for the constitution to be written after those elections, not before. Both demands, if met, would have closed Bremer's privatization window. Then, on March 2, with the Shia members of the Governing Council refusing to sign the interim constitution, five bombs exploded in front of mosques in Karbala and Baghdad, killing close to two hundred worshippers. General John Abizaid, the top U.S. commander in Iraq, warned that the country was on the verge of civil war. Frightened by this prospect, al Sistani backed down and the Shia politicians signed the interim constitution. It was a familiar story: the shock of a violent attack paved the way for more shock therapy.

When I arrived in Iraq a week later, the economic project seemed to be back on track. All that remained for Bremer was to get his interim constitution ratified by a UN Security Council resolution, then the nervous lawyers and insurance brokers could relax and the sell-off of Iraq could finally begin. The CPA, meanwhile, had launched a major new PR offensive designed to reassure investors that Iraq was still a safe and exciting place to do business. The centrepiece of the campaign was Destination Baghdad Exposition, a massive trade show for potential investors to be held in early April at the Baghdad International Fairgrounds. It was the first such event inside Iraq, and the organizers had branded the trade fair "DBX," as if it were some sort of Mountain Dew–sponsored dirt-bike race. In keeping with the extreme-sports theme, Thomas Foley travelled to Washington to tell a gathering of executives that the risks in Iraq are akin "to skydiving or riding a motorcycle, which are, to many, very acceptable risks."

But three hours after my arrival in Baghdad, I was finding these reassurances extremely hard to believe. I had not yet unpacked when my hotel room was filled with debris and the windows in the lobby were shattered. Down the street, the Mount Lebanon Hotel had just been bombed, at that point the largest attack of its kind since the official end of the war. The next day, another hotel was bombed in Basra, then two Finnish businessmen were murdered on their way to a meeting in Baghdad. Brig. Gen. Mark Kimmitt finally admitted that there was a pattern at work: "the extremists have started shifting away from the hard targets...and are now going out of their way to specifically target softer targets." The next day, the State Department updated its travel advisory: U.S. citizens were "strongly warned against travel to Iraq." The physical risks of doing business in Iraq seemed to be spiralling out of control. This, once again, was not part of the original plan. When Bremer first arrived in Baghdad, the armed resistance was so low that he was able to walk the streets with a minimal security entourage. During his first four months on the job, 109 U.S. soldiers were killed and 570 were wounded. In the following four months, when Bremer's shock therapy had taken effect, the number of U.S. casualties almost doubled, with 195 soldiers killed and 1,633 wounded. There are many in Iraq who argue that these events are connected —that Bremer's reforms were the single largest factor leading to the rise of armed resistance.

Take, for instance, Bremer's first casualties. The soldiers and workers he laid off without pensions or severance pay didn't all disappear quietly. Many of them went straight into the mujahedeen, forming the backbone of the armed resistance. "Half a million people are now worse off, and there you have the water tap that keeps the insurgency going. It's alternative employment," says Hussain Kubba, head of the prominent Iraqi business group Kubba Consulting. Some of Bremer's other economic casualties also have failed to go quietly. It turns out that many of the businessmen whose companies are threatened by Bremer's investment laws have decided to make investments of their own — in the resistance. It is partly their money that keeps fighters in Kalashnikovs and RPGs.

These developments present a challenge to the basic logic of shock therapy: the neocons were convinced that if they brought in their reforms quickly and ruthlessly, Iraqis would be too stunned to resist. But the shock appears to have had the opposite effect; rather than the predicted paralysis, it jolted many Iraqis into action, much of it extreme. Haider al-Abadi, Iraq's minister of communication, puts it this way: "We know that there are terrorists in the country, but previously they were not successful, they were isolated. Now because the whole country is unhappy, and a lot of people don't have jobs...these terrorists are finding listening ears."

Bremer was now at odds not only with the Iraqis who opposed his plans but with U.S. military commanders charged with putting down the insurgency his policies were feeding. Heretical questions began to be raised: instead of laying people off, what if the CPA actually created jobs for Iraqis? And instead of rushing to sell off Iraq's two hundred state-owned firms, how about putting them back to work?

From the start, the neocons running Iraq had shown nothing but disdain for Iraq's state-owned companies. In keeping with their Year Zero–apocalyptic glee, when looters descended on the factories during the war, U.S. forces did nothing. Sabah Asaad, managing director of a refrigerator factory outside Baghdad, told me that while the looting was going on, he went to a nearby U.S. Army base and begged for help. "I asked one of the officers to send two soldiers and a vehicle to help me kick out the looters. I was crying. The officer said, 'Sorry, we can't do anything, we need an order from President Bush.'" Back in Washington, Donald Rumsfeld shrugged. "Free people are free to make mistakes and commit crimes and do bad things."

To see the remains of Asaad's football-field-size warehouse is to understand why Frank Gehry had an artistic crisis after September 11 and was briefly unable to design structures resembling the rubble of modern buildings. Asaad's looted and burned factory looks remarkably like a heavy-metal version of Gehry's Guggenheim in Bilbao, Spain, with waves of steel, buckled by fire, lying in terrifyingly beautiful golden heaps. Yet all was not lost. "The looters were good-hearted," one of Asaad's painters told me, explaining that they left the tools and machines behind, "so we could work again." Because the machines are still there, many factory managers in Iraq say that it would take little for them to return to full production. They need emergency generators to cope with daily blackouts, and they need capital for parts and raw materials. If that happened, it would have tremendous implications for Iraq's stalled reconstruction, because it would mean that many of the key materials needed to rebuild — cement and steel, bricks and furniture — could be produced inside the country.

But it hasn't happened. Immediately after the nominal end of the war, Congress appropriated $2.5 billion for the reconstruction of Iraq, followed by an additional $18.4 billion in October. Yet as of July 2004, Iraq's state-owned factories had been pointedly excluded from the reconstruction contracts. Instead, the billions have all gone to Western companies, with most of the materials for the reconstruction imported at great expense from abroad.

With unemployment as high as sixty-seven percent, the imported products and foreign workers flooding across the borders have become a source of tremendous resentment in Iraq and yet another open tap fuelling the insurgency. And Iraqis don't have to look far for reminders of this injustice; it's on display in the most ubiquitous symbol of the occupation: the blast wall. The ten-foot-high slabs of reinforced concrete are everywhere in Iraq, separating the protected — the people in upscale hotels, luxury homes, military bases, and, of course, the Green Zone — from the unprotected and exposed. If that wasn't enough, all the blast walls are imported, from Kurdistan, Turkey, or even farther afield, this despite the fact that Iraq was once a major manufacturer of cement, and could easily be again. There are seventeen state-owned cement factories across the country, but most are idle or working at only half capacity. According to the Ministry of Industry, not one of these factories has received a single contract to help with the reconstruction, even though they could produce the walls and meet other needs for cement at a greatly reduced cost. The CPA pays up to $1,000 per imported blast wall; local manufacturers say they could make them for $100. Minister Tofiq says there is a simple reason why the Americans refuse to help get Iraq's cement factories running again: among those making the decision, "no one believes in the public sector." (Tofiq did say that several U.S. companies had expressed strong interest in buying the state-owned cement factories. This supports a widely held belief in Iraq that there is a deliberate strategy to neglect the state firms so that they can be sold more cheaply — a practice known as "starve then sell.")

This kind of ideological blindness has turned Iraq's occupiers into prisoners of their own policies, hiding behind walls that, by their very existence, fuel the rage at the U.S. presence, thereby feeding the need for more walls. In Baghdad the concrete barriers have been given a popular nickname: Bremer walls.

As the insurgency grew, it soon became clear that if Bremer went ahead with his plans to sell off the state companies, it could worsen the violence. There was no question that privatization would require layoffs: the Ministry of Industry estimates that roughly 145,000 workers would have to be fired to make the firms desirable to investors, with each of those workers supporting, on average, five family members. For Iraq's besieged occupiers the question was, would these shock-therapy casualties accept their fate or would they rebel?

The answer arrived, in rather dramatic fashion, at one of the largest state-owned companies, the General Company for Vegetable Oils. The complex of six factories produces cooking oil, hand soap, laundry detergent, shaving cream, and shampoo. At least that is what I was told by a receptionist who gave me glossy brochures and calendars boasting of "modern instruments" and "the latest and most up-to-date developments in the field of industry." But when I approached the soap factory, I discovered a group of workers sleeping outside a darkened building. Our guide rushed ahead, shouting something to a woman in a white lab coat, and suddenly the factory scrambled into activity: lights switched on, motors revved up, and workers — still blinking off sleep — began filling two-litre plastic bottles with pale blue Zahi brand dishwashing liquid.

I asked Nada Ahmed, the woman in the white coat, why the factory wasn't working a few minutes before. She explained that they have only enough electricity and materials to run the machines for a couple of hours a day, but when guests arrive — would-be investors, ministry officials, journalists — they get them going. "For show," she explained. Behind us, a dozen bulky machines sat idle, covered in sheets of dusty plastic and secured with duct tape.

In one dark corner of the plant, we came across an old man hunched over a sack filled with white plastic caps. With a thin metal blade lodged in a wedge of wax, he carefully whittled down the edges of each cap, leaving a pile of shavings at his feet. "We don't have the spare part for the proper mould, so we have to cut them by hand," his supervisor explained apologetically. "We haven't received any parts from Germany since the sanctions began." I noticed that even on the assembly lines that were nominally working there was almost no mechanization: bottles were held under spouts by hand because conveyor belts don't convey, lids once snapped on by machines were being hammered in place with wooden mallets. Even the water for the factory was drawn from an outdoor well, hoisted by hand, and carried inside.

The solution proposed by the U.S. occupiers was not to fix the plant but to sell it, and so when Bremer announced the privatization auction back in June 2003 this was among the first companies mentioned. Yet when I visited the factory in March, nobody wanted to talk about the privatization plan; the mere mention of the word inside the plant inspired awkward silences and meaningful glances. This seemed an unnatural amount of subtext for a soap factory, and I tried to get to the bottom of it when I interviewed the assistant manager. But the interview itself was equally odd: I had spent half a week setting it up, submitting written questions for approval, getting a signed letter of permission from the minister of industry, being questioned and searched several times. But when I finally began the interview, the assistant manager refused to tell me his name or let me record the conversation. "Any manager mentioned in the press is attacked afterwards," he said. And when I asked whether the company was being sold, he gave this oblique response. "If the decision was up to the workers, they are against privatization; but if it's up to the high-ranking officials and government, then privatization is an order and orders must be followed."

I left the plant feeling that I knew less than when I'd arrived. But on the way out of the gates, a young security guard handed my translator a note. He wanted us to meet him after work at a nearby restaurant, "to find out what is really going on with privatization." His name was Mahmud, and he was a twenty five year old with a neat beard and big black eyes. (For his safety, I have omitted his last name.) His story began in July, a few weeks after Bremer's privatization announcement. The company's manager, on his way to work, was shot to death. Press reports speculated that the manager was murdered because he was in favour of privatizing the plant, but Mahmud was convinced that he was killed because he opposed the plan. "He would never have sold the factories like the Americans want. That's why they killed him."

The dead man was replaced by a new manager, Mudhfar Ja'far. Shortly after taking over, Ja'far called a meeting with ministry officials to discuss selling off the soap factory, which would involve laying off two-thirds of its employees. Guarding that meeting were several security officers from the plant. They listened closely to Ja'far's plans and promptly reported the alarming news to their coworkers. "We were shocked," Mahmud recalled. "If the private sector buys our company, the first thing they would do is reduce the staff to make more money. And we will be forced into a very hard destiny, because the factory is our only way of living."

Frightened by this prospect, a group of seventeen workers, including Mahmud, marched into Ja'far's office to confront him on what they had heard. "Unfortunately, he wasn't there, only the assistant manager, the one you met," Mahmud told me. A fight broke out: one worker struck the assistant manager, and a bodyguard fired three shots at the workers. The crowd then attacked the bodyguard, took his gun, and, Mahmud said, "stabbed him with a knife in the back three times. He spent a month in the hospital." In January there was even more violence. On their way to work, Ja'far, the manager, and his son were shot and badly injured. Mahmud told me he had no idea who was behind the attack, but I was starting to understand why factory managers in Iraq try to keep a low profile.

At the end of our meeting, I asked Mahmud what would happen if the plant was sold despite the workers' objections. "There are two choices," he said, looking me in the eye and smiling kindly. "Either we will set the factory on fire and let the flames devour it to the ground, or we will blow ourselves up inside of it. But it will not be privatized."

If there ever was a moment when Iraqis were too disoriented to resist shock therapy, that moment has definitely passed. Labour relations, like everything else in Iraq, has become a blood sport. The violence on the streets howls at the gates of the factories, threatening to engulf them. Workers fear job loss as a death sentence, and managers, in turn, fear their workers, a fact that makes privatization distinctly more complicated than the neocons foresaw. (It is in Basra where the connections between economic reforms and the rise of the resistance was put in starkest terms. In December, the union representing oil workers was negotiating with the Oil Ministry for a salary increase. Getting nowhere, the workers offered the ministry a simple choice: increase their paltry salaries or they would all join the armed resistance. They received a substantial raise.)

As I left the meeting with Mahmud, I got word that there was a major demonstration outside the CPA headquarters. Supporters of the radical young cleric Moqtada al Sadr were protesting the closing of their newspaper, *al Hawza*, by military police. The CPA accused *al Hawza* of publishing "false articles" that could "pose the real threat of violence." As an example, it cited an article that claimed Bremer "is pursuing a policy of starving the Iraqi people to make them preoccupied with procuring their daily bread so they do not have the chance to demand their political and individual freedoms." To me it sounded less like hate literature than a concise summary of Milton Friedman's recipe for shock therapy.

A few days before the newspaper was shut down, I had gone to Kufa during Friday prayers to listen to al Sadr at his mosque. He had launched into a tirade against Bremer's newly signed interim constitution, calling it "an unjust, terrorist document." The message of the sermon was clear: Grand Ayatollah Ali al Sistani may have backed down on the constitution, but al Sadr and his supporters were still determined to fight it — and if they succeeded they would sabotage the neocons' careful plan to saddle

Iraq's next government with their "wish list" of laws. With the closing of the newspaper, Bremer was giving al Sadr his response: he wasn't negotiating with this young upstart; he'd rather take him out with force.

When I arrived at the demonstration, the streets were filled with men dressed in black, the soon-to-be legendary Mahdi Army. It struck me that if Mahmud lost his security guard job at the soap factory, he could be one of them. That's who al Sadr's foot soldiers are: the young men who have been shut out of the neocons' grand plans for Iraq, who see no possibilities for work, and whose neighbourhoods have seen none of the promised reconstruction. Bremer has failed these young men, and everywhere that he has failed, Moqtada al Sadr has cannily set out to succeed. In Shia slums from Baghdad to Basra, a network of Sadr Centres coordinate a kind of shadow reconstruction. Funded through donations, the centres dispatch electricians to fix power and phone lines, organize local garbage collection, set up emergency generators, run blood drives, direct traffic where the streetlights don't work. And yes, they organize militias too. Al Sadr took Bremer's economic casualties, dressed them in black, and gave them rusty Kalashnikovs. His militiamen protected the mosques and the state factories when the occupation authorities did not, but in some areas they also went further, zealously enforcing Islamic law by torching liquor stores and terrorizing women without the veil. Indeed, the astronomical rise of the brand of religious fundamentalism that al Sadr represents is another kind of blowback from Bremer's shock therapy: if the reconstruction had provided jobs, security, and services to Iraqis, al Sadr would have been deprived of both his mission and many of his newfound followers.

At the same time as al Sadr's followers were shouting "Down with America" outside the Green Zone, something was happening in another part of the country that would change everything. Four American mercenary soldiers were killed in Fallujah, their charred and dismembered bodies hung like trophies over the Euphrates. The attacks would prove a devastating blow for the neocons, one from which they would never recover. With these images, investing in Iraq suddenly didn't look anything like a capitalist dream; it looked like a macabre nightmare made real.

The day I left Baghdad was the worst yet. Fallujah was under siege and Brig. Gen. Kimmitt was threatening to "destroy the al-Mahdi army." By the end, roughly two thousand Iraqis were killed in those twin campaigns. I was dropped off at a security checkpoint several miles from the airport, then loaded onto a bus jammed with contractors lugging hastily packed bags. Although no one was calling it one, this was an evacuation: over the next week 1,500 contractors left Iraq, and some governments began airlifting their citizens out of the country. On the bus no one spoke; we all just listened to the mortar fire, craning our necks to see the red glow. A guy carrying a KPMG briefcase decided to lighten things up. "So is there business class on this flight?" he asked the silent bus. From the back, somebody called out, "Not yet."

Indeed, it may be quite a while before business class truly arrives in Iraq. When we landed in Amman, we learned that we had gotten out just in time. That morning three Japanese civilians were kidnapped and their captors were threatening to burn them alive. Two days later Nicholas Berg went missing and was not seen again until the snuff film surfaced of his beheading, an even more terrifying message for U.S. contractors than the charred bodies in Fallujah. These were the start of a wave of kidnappings and killings of foreigners, most of them businesspeople, from a rainbow of nations: South Korea, Italy, China, Nepal, Pakistan, the Philippines, Turkey. By the end of June more than ninety contractors were reported dead in Iraq. When seven Turkish contractors were kidnapped in June, their captors asked the "company to cancel all contracts and pull out employees from Iraq." Many insurance companies stopped selling life insurance to contractors, and others began to charge premiums as high as $10,000 a week for a single Western executive — the same price some insurgents reportedly pay for a dead American.

For their part, the organizers of DBX, the historic Baghdad trade fair, decided to relocate to the lovely tourist city of Diyarbakir in Turkey, "just 250 kilometres from the Iraqi border." An Iraqi landscape, only without those frightening Iraqis. Three weeks later just fifteen people showed up for a Commerce Department conference in Lansing, Michigan, on investing in Iraq. Its host, Republican Congressman Mike Rogers, tried to reassure his skeptical audience by saying that Iraq is "like a rough neighborhood anywhere in America." The foreign investors, the ones who were offered every imaginable free-market enticement, are clearly not convinced; there is still no sign of them. Keith Crane, a senior economist at the RAND Corporation who has worked for the CPA, put it bluntly: "I don't believe the board of a multinational company could approve a major investment in this environment. If people are shooting at each other, it's just difficult to do business." Hamid Jassim Khamis, the manager of the largest soft-drink bottling plant in the region, told me he can't find any investors, even though he landed the exclusive rights to produce Pepsi in central Iraq. "A lot of people have approached us to invest in the factory, but people are really hesitating now." Khamis said he couldn't blame them; in five months he has survived an attempted assassination, a carjacking, two bombs planted at the entrance of his factory, and the kidnapping of his son.

Despite having been granted the first licence for a foreign bank to operate in Iraq in forty years, HSBC still hasn't opened any branches, a decision that may mean losing the coveted licence altogether. Procter & Gamble has put its joint venture on hold, and so has General Motors. The U.S. financial backers of the Starwood luxury hotel and multiplex have gotten cold feet, and Siemens AG has pulled most staff from Iraq. The bell hasn't rung yet at the Baghdad Stock Exchange — in fact you can't even use credit cards in Iraq's cash-only economy. New Bridge Strategies, the company that had gushed, back in October, about how "a Wal-Mart could take over the country," sounding distinctly humbled. "McDonald's is not opening anytime soon," company partner Ed Rogers told the *Washington Post*. Neither is Wal-Mart. The *Financial Times* has declared Iraq "the most dangerous place in the world in which to do business." It's quite an accomplishment: in trying to design the best place in the world to do business, the neocons have managed to create the worst, the most eloquent indictment yet of the guiding logic behind deregulated free markets.

The violence has not just kept investors out; it also forced Bremer, before he left, to abandon many of his central economic policies. Privatization of the state companies is off the table; instead, several of the state companies have been offered up for lease, but only if the investor agrees not to lay off a single employee. Thousands of the state workers that Bremer fired have been rehired, and significant raises have been handed out in the public sector as a whole. Plans to do away with the food-ration program have also been scrapped — it just doesn't seem like a good time to deny millions of Iraqis the only nutrition on which they can depend.

The final blow to the neocon dream came in the weeks before the handover. The White House and the CPA were rushing to get the U.N. Security Council to pass a resolution endorsing their handover plan. They had twisted arms to give the top job to former CIA agent Iyad Allawi, a move that will ensure that Iraq becomes, at the very least, the coaling station for U.S. troops that Jay Garner originally envisioned. But if major corporate investors were going to come to Iraq in the future, they would need a stronger guarantee that Bremer's economic laws would stick. There was only one way of doing that: the Security Council resolution had to ratify the interim constitution, which locked in Bremer's laws for the duration of the interim government. But al Sistani once again objected, this time unequivocally, saying that the constitution has been "rejected by the majority of the Iraqi people." On June 8 the Security Council unanimously passed a resolution that endorsed the handover plan but made absolutely no reference to the constitution. In the face of this far-reaching defeat, George W. Bush celebrated the resolution as a historic victory, one that came just in time for an election trail photo-op at the G8 Summit in Georgia.

With Bremer's laws in limbo, Iraqi ministers are already talking openly about breaking contracts signed by the CPA. Citigroup's loan scheme has been rejected as a misuse of Iraq's oil revenues. Iraq's communication minister is threatening to renegotiate contracts with the three communications firms providing the country with its disastrously poor cellphone service. And the Lebanese and U.S. companies hired to run the state television network have been informed that they could lose their licences because they are not Iraqi. "We will see if we can change the contract," Hamid al-Kifaey, spokesperson for the Governing Council, said in May. "They have no idea about Iraq." For most investors, this complete lack of legal certainty simply makes Iraq too great a risk.

But while the Iraqi resistance has managed to scare off the first wave of corporate raiders, there's little doubt that they will return. Whatever form the next Iraqi government takes — nationalist, Islamist, or free market — it will inherit a crushing $120 billion debt. Then, as in all poor countries around the world, men in dark blue suits from the IMF will appear at the door, bearing loans and promises of economic boom, provided that certain structural adjustments are made, which will, of course, be rather painful at first but well worth the sacrifice in the end. In fact, the process has already begun: the IMF is poised to approve loans worth $2.5 to $4.25 billion, pending agreement on the conditions. After an endless succession of courageous last stands and far too many lost lives, Iraq will become a poor nation like any other, with politicians determined to introduce policies rejected by the vast majority of the population, and all the imperfect compromises that will entail. The free market will no doubt come to Iraq, but the neoconservative dream of transforming the country into a free-market utopia has already died, a casualty of a greater dream — a second term for George W. Bush.

The great historical irony of the catastrophe unfolding in Iraq is that the shock-therapy reforms that were supposed to create an economic boom that would rebuild the country instead fuelled a resistance that ultimately made reconstruction impossible. Bremer's reforms unleashed forces that the neocons neither predicted nor could hope to control, from armed insurrections inside factories to tens of thousands of unemployed young men arming themselves. These forces have transformed Year Zero in Iraq into the mirror opposite of what the neocons envisioned: not a corporate utopia but a ghoulish dystopia, where going to a simple business meeting can get you lynched, burned alive, or beheaded. These dangers are so great that in Iraq global capitalism has retreated, at least for now. For the neocons, this must be a shocking development: their ideological belief in greed turns out to be stronger than greed itself.

Iraq was to the neocons what Afghanistan was to the Taliban: the one place on earth where they could force everyone to live by the most literal, unyielding interpretation of their sacred texts. One would think that the bloody results of this experiment would inspire a crisis of faith: in the country where they had absolute free reign, where there was no local government to blame, where economic reforms were introduced at their most shocking and most perfect, they created, instead of a model free market, a failed state no right-thinking investor would touch. And yet the Green Zone neocons and their masters in Washington are no more likely to re-examine their core beliefs than the Taliban mullahs were inclined to search their souls when their Islamic state slid into a debauched Hades of opium and sex slavery. When facts threaten true believers, they simply close their eyes and pray harder.

Which is precisely what Thomas Foley has been doing. The former head of "private sector development" has left Iraq, a country he had described as "the mother of all turnarounds," and has accepted another turnaround job, as co-chair of George Bush's re-election committee in Connecticut. On April 30 in Washington he addressed a crowd of entrepreneurs about business prospects in Baghdad. It was a tough day to be giving an upbeat speech: that morning the first photographs had appeared out of Abu Ghraib, including one of a hooded prisoner with electrical wires attached to his hands. This was another kind of shock therapy, far more literal than the one Foley had helped to administer, but not entirely unconnected. "Whatever you're seeing, it's not as bad as it appears," Foley told the crowd. "You just need to accept that on faith."

October 28, 2004

ROY MacGREGOR

Witness to a Country

In the fall of 2006, Roy MacGregor, veteran newspaperman, magazine writer, and author of books, came to campus. Since 2002, MacGregor had been writing columns for the Globe and Mail, *but he had a long and distinguished career in hand before he came to the national newspaper. He had won National Newspaper Awards, National Magazine Awards, and in 2005 was named an officer in the Order of Canada. He is the author of more than 40 books — 28 of them in the internationally successful* Screech Owls *mystery series for young readers — on subjects ranging from Canada, to the James Bay Cree, to hockey. That fall, he spoke to a packed room in the St. Thomas chapel. After the lecture, Herménégilde Chiasson, the Acadian poet, artist, and New Brunswick's Lieutenant Governor of the day, hosted a reception at the majestic Old Government House on the banks of the St. John River. MacGregor spent the evening surrounded by young journalists and the conversation continued late into the night. After all, there were more than three decades of stories to tell.*

Whenever I think of Dalton Camp, I am reminded of a line of his that has stuck with me ever since I first read in his marvellous *Points of Departure* back in 1979: "Over his breakfast of Gravol and coffee later that morning, the varlet brooded upon the events of the night before."

The "night before" had been the parliamentary press gallery dinner. Having been there, I could empathize. I have carried Gravol with me ever since.

I never met Dalton Camp. Not that night, not after, but over the years I listened to him on CBC Radio and read him in Canadian newspapers. His column ran in the *Toronto Star*, where he was often identified by the baggage he carried. "Dalton Camp is a former president of the Progressive Conservative Party of Canada" or "Dalton Camp was a senior adviser to the federal government from 1986 to 1989." The *Star* closed his columnist days out with, "Dalton Camp is a political commentator and broadcaster."

I would have said, "Dalton Camp is a writer living in New Brunswick." Or, perhaps more accurately, "living and working in 'Camp's Corner,' DJ Purdy's [bar], Sheraton Hotel, Fredericton, New Brunswick."

He was not only a writer, but a truly great writer. And it has always struck me as oddly Canadian — in the very country that, like the bumblebee, simply defies logic — that the finest practitioner of one of the official languages was not from among our novelists, not from our short story writers, not even from the traditional magazine feature writers or newspaper columnists. Instead, he was a writer who had come up through the slippery language of politics and the sneaky syntax of advertising. However he got to where he ended up, he made the best of it, and wrote with a clarity to which the rest of us can only aspire.

June Callwood, who gave the very first lecture in this series back in 2002, said Dalton Camp never intended to end his days writing for a newspaper. "It happened for two good reasons," June Callwood said, "both of which I suggest are the essence of fine journalism. One is that he had something to say and the other is that he knew how to say it well. And it wasn't such a transformation at all for him to move from politician to journalist, because journalism stands at the heart of democracy."

Later, I hope to return to this line: "Journalism stands at the heart of democracy."

Dalton Camp never went to journalism school. I did. But not one like this one at St. Thomas University. I took a year of post-graduate journalism that, mercifully, has since been deep-sixed by the Ontario university that offered it.

I will tell you about only one class: magazine writing. Since the professor who taught it so desperately craved recognition, I will, if you don't mind, deny him his wish. He shall have no name here.

This professor of journalism believed magazine journalism existed only to separate the ads, and that the real messages lay in embedded subliminal tricks designed to get readers to purchase products they didn't want or need. He found naked orgies in liquor ads. He found imbedded erections in clothing ads. He once blew up a *Playboy* cover to show how the model's hair had been twisted into letters spelling out a highly suggestive sexual invitation to those fine young men who might be browsing the magazine racks in search of, say, a good magazine on model airplanes.

One day, in a moment of great triumph, he claimed to have found the word "sex" imbedded exactly sixty-nine times in the breakfast placemats of the local Howard Johnson's. For weeks, he had found himself showing up for identical orders of pancakes and sausages and — until this amazing discovery — had not understood where such cravings came from. Now he did.

He had no trouble swallowing pancakes and sausages; we had trouble swallowing anything he said.

This very strange man gave us three assignments that year: one, men write for a men's magazine, women write for one of those Hollywood fan magazines; two, everyone write the horoscope for *Cosmopolitan*; and three, defend Canada's defence policy in the pages of *Chatelaine*. One mischievous member of our class wrote to editor Doris Anderson pitching this positively splendid idea and got a form letter back that may or may not have said, "Are you out of your tree?"

Yet it was not, as some may be thinking, a lost year. I lost all fear that journalism might be some secret handshake ever to be denied me. Surely if some of these incompetents were *teaching* journalism, I would be able to *do* journalism. I have also, over the years, become increasingly convinced that there is much more to successful journalism than what can be taught. Technique is important, of course, but a part of you needs to be a born journalist.

There is no class on the journalist personality, but it does exist. It is a rare successful practitioner of this trade who has not thought that one day someone important is going to come to you, place an arm around the shoulder, and say: "Look, we don't know how you did it — and in a way we kind of even admire you for it — but we're on to you now. We know you're a complete fake and a fraud. If you agree to go away quietly, we'll not say anything publicly to embarrass you."

I would actually suggest that insecurity is a significant tool in successful journalism. It makes you work harder. It makes you crave recognition. It makes you doubt yourself, meaning you will check and check again. It makes you listen carefully, anxious not to miss anything. And it makes you want to do better next time. And next time. And next time.

This journalist personality is most on display at social events, not in newsrooms. Journalists, in awkward situations, tend to fall back on the only real social skill they possess: interviewing people. It's sort of a harmless social tic. The people most journalists talk to at parties tend to go away convinced you're one of the most interesting people they have ever met, when in fact all you've been is the most-interested person they encountered that evening. All you could think to do was ask questions about them, and people love nothing better than to talk about themselves. Not once, of course, did it occur to them to ask a question back.

I also think that the curse of the education system — attention-deficit — is the great blessing of the journalist. Three of our four children "suffer" — and I use that term loosely — from ADHD, and for years I have asked them the same two questions. One, how come you never again hear about the person who stands first in the class? And two, why is it that almost every remarkably successful person you hear about is said to have "the attention span of a butterfly?"

It is interesting, no, that while school caters to those who can sit still, the world opens to those who cannot. And journalists, good journalists, can't sit still — except, of course, when they're listening to an absolutely captivating lecture.

Journalism is a privileged life, just so long as you keep in mind that it is your byline that is opening the doors and not your name.

I learned two valuable life lessons years ago from Mordecai Richler. It was very early in my career and I had been sent off by *Maclean's* magazine to profile the great writer, then about to bring out a new novel. We met at the Montreal Press Club, where he pressed several drinks upon me, and then headed up to the apartment he shared on Sherbrooke Street with his wife Florence. He stopped on the way and purchased two bottles — full forty-ounces — of Rémy Martin.

I had brought along a tape recorder, one of those old portable ones about the size of a laptop. I had brought it along, I believed at the time, solely for legal protection, wary of Richler's great reputation for surliness. I checked the batteries, set up the tiny microphone, and pushed "record" before turning to my carefully prepared "prep" notes.

The decision to tape was the smartest, perhaps luckiest, thing I ever did in journalism. The prep notes went out the window. Richler, who was not in the least testy, wasn't interested in predictable questions. He was somewhat eager to talk, but particularly eager to get into the Rémy. He would pour a large drink for himself, then a small one for me and push it over. Being a beer drinker, I accepted largely out of politeness.

He began to talk of his life as a writer. I began to spin. I woke up on my hotel room bed, still wearing the clothes I had worn to the interview. I had not before, and have not since, felt such panic about a story. I had completely screwed up. My career was over.

Head throbbing, stomach churning, I checked around the room and finally noticed the tape recorder. Deep in prayer, I scrambled over, pressed rewind, waited breathlessly and then, heart pounding, pressed down the play button.

Richler's voice came through loud and clear. I flipped the tape over and pressed play again and heard my voice, slurring, nonsensical. Richler's voice, still loud and clear without so much as a slur — well, at least, not in the way in which he spoke. As I listened, seemingly for the first time, I realized we were talking about journalism, not novel writing, and he was explaining why he turned so often to journalism. He needed material, he said. He needed access.

And journalism, Mordecai Richler said, "gives me *entrée* into worlds I could not otherwise be a part of." How true. How true. Looking back on more than three decades of journalism, most of it spent running around this impossible and impossibly huge country, usually alone, I have myself sometimes felt a bit of this outsider-insider sensation.

For me, it has been more Woody Allen's *Zelig* than Tom Hanks's *Forrest Gump,* in that you are there as witness but not really there as participant — even if largely by accident, as in the case of the fictional Gump. It has always felt more Zelig in that you tend to be always in the picture, invariably in the background, and no one is ever quite sure who you are or how you got there. *Entrée,* into worlds you could not otherwise be a part of. Once you get there, however, you really have to know where to look. And what to listen for.

In the fall of 2000, I was on a train moving between Ottawa and Montreal. It was, at times, moving very slowly, as also on board was the body of Pierre Trudeau, former prime minister of Canada. The few journalists allowed on board were kept to a separate car, and every so often a senator or former colleague would be brought up and sat down so we could record his thoughts on this moment. But the story wasn't in the car at all. It was unfolding on the other side of the window.

I finally realized this as our train, Via Rail no. 638, neared Casselman. We were passing a field, and there was a farmer standing dead centre in his field beside his tractor. An older man, wearing rust-coloured coveralls and high green rubber boots. And was standing at attention. When the train passed, he took off his cap and very slowly saluted.

There were such scenes all along the route. In one small village, it was the volunteer fire brigade, in full uniform, all at attention on one side of the tracks while on the other stood a peewee hockey team, also in uniform, also at attention.

Golfers stepped back from putts and took off their caps.

At one crossing, a woman held up a cherry paddle, a rainbow-coloured *voyageur* scarf tied carefully around it. At another, a man held up his country's flag with his country's perfect flagpole, a hockey stick.

A railway worker stood to the side of the tracks, his hardhat cradled in his left arm while he stood at attention.

People who had been waiting at crossings in lawn chairs stood and cheered. Youngsters sat in trees and waved small flags. Older couples pulled their cars over onto gravel shoulders, got out, and stood silently at attention as the slow train passed.

Near the outskirts of little Alexandria, something else began to happen. The train jerked and lost speed, then shuddered to slower still.

What had happened was that, as no. 638, began passing through Alexandria, the crowd, six and eight people deep in places, pushed forward.

Boy Scouts and Girl Guides at attention were squeezed until they were forced to stutter-step closer. The aging members of the local branch of the Royal Canadian Legion — chests out, service medals flashing — were forced to edge closer, the small corps of young cadets lined up beside the Legionnaires following suit as the growing crowd pushed ever closer to the slowing train.

Through the glass, we could hear a single piper playing *The Last Post*. The train slowed to a bare crawl.

And this was when we heard The Hands of Alexandria.

I was standing beside New Brunswick's Jim Munson, now a senator but then still reporting for CTV News. We couldn't figure out what the sound was — this growing, rubbery squeak.

Not the wheels. Not the brakes. But something else. And then we realized what it was: *skin*.

The people of Alexandria were reaching out to touch the train. They were, literally, feeling the passing of Pierre Elliott Trudeau, their hands rubbing along the metal of the cars as the train slowly made its way through the small town.

Munson and I stood at the window, staring down at hundreds of hands — some so young they had to reach up, some so old they shook helplessly — reaching out to touch the funeral train. Their faces, many openly weeping, were the faces of Canada, every age, both sexes, both languages, old Canadians and young Canadians, old Canadians and new Canadians, all reaching out to touch the train that was carrying Pierre Trudeau to his grave.

Jim Munson broke down first. But he was not alone.

I do not believe I have heard anything quite so moving as the sound of the skin of Canada on the history of Canada. It sent chills up and down the spines of every person in the funeral car and still, today, sends chills up and down my spine to remember that oddly mouse-like sound that baffled us until we figured out what was happening in Alexandria.

But there was more to it than just confusion. It was the surprise — there is no other word for it — of staring out at a country and seeing a face that you had no idea was there, even though your job, day in and day out, is to describe this face and give it voice. It was also the stark realization we were staring out at one small corner of a country so large it defies generalities, defies, we sometimes think, even slight understanding.

Staring out at Canada, and yet acutely, startlingly aware that if Via Rail no. 638 — the funeral train carrying former Prime Minister Pierre Elliott Trudeau — happened this same soft October day to be passing through, say Salmon Arm, British Columbia, rather than Alexandria, Ontario, the people of Canada would still be reaching out.

But not to touch the train; rather, to give the finger.

I have now spent more than thirty years interviewing this country, and the more questions I ask, the more questions arise. The more I travel, the more I realize how little I have seen. The harder I stare, the less I see as clearly as I thought I had. Mordecai Richler's *entrée* has taken me to places I never thought to be and, had I thought, would think I had no right to be. That's why it's always important to remember it's the byline the door opens for, not the name.

That byline got to: try Nashville with Ian Tyson; stay on an oil rig off the coast of Newfoundland; attend Rocket Richard's funeral; be at the Oka standoff; travel to Alert Bay with the Governor General; barnstorm around Europe with Wayne Gretzky while the National Hockey League was shut down; live with the Crees of James Bay; watch Elijah Harper Jr. put an end to the Meech Lake Accord.

The faces that light up most brightly, however, are not among those familiar names, despite their high currency at social gatherings, on the off chance that the person I'm "interviewing" might think to squeeze a return question in.

The ones I treasure are those people who are rarely, if ever, interviewed, people with no sense of persona or clip or even how their words and actions will appear, if indeed they appear at all. They have simply agreed to talk, or let you in to their lives for a short while, and it is this *entrée*, this remarkable privilege of seeing people at the core of their existence, that stays forever.

In the past couple of years alone I have been honoured to spend time with Betty Fitzgerald, the mayor of Bonavista, and listen to this former nurse plot out how her lovely little town on the eastern shore of Newfoundland need not disappear just because the cod has.

I have sat with Gerald Merkel, a young farmer in Raymore, Saskatchewan, and heard him talk about the farm accident in which he almost killed his father and then the frost that came along and killed his uninsured crop — "She's beyond crying" — and sat dumbfounded as he mapped out planting plans for the coming season, banks willing.

I have sipped coffee in Saskatoon, with Matthew Dunn, a brilliant mechanical engineering graduate and National Aboriginal Achievement Award winner who hopes to become an astronaut.

I have been invited by Shirley Chan into the basement of her Vancouver home to see the small shrine she built to her mother, Lee Wo Soon Chan, who well into her eighties was known as "The Mayor of Chinatown" and left behind a sense of pride and belonging that was most assuredly not there when she first arrived in this country.

I have stood at the foot of the large statue to Marie-Madeleine Jarret de Verchères that stares out from the south shore of the St. Lawrence River and listened to young Marie-Eve Lainesse talk about how her generation has given up on politics but never for a moment on who they are and where they live.

I have sat with Don Bogstie, a big, retired farmer in British Columbia's Shuswap region who happily calls himself a "redneck" and listened while he explained why he would be "honoured" to witness the same-sex marriage of the two girls on the farm across the road — "so long as I don't have to wear a tie."

I have sat in a tanning shed in the small Dogrib community of Behchoko, Northwest Territories, and watched eighty-year-old Elisabeth Chocolate use a tool fashioned from the leg bone of a caribou to scrape away the fat from beaver pelts brought in by her son-in-law, Patrick Adzin, who will leave the next day for the far barrens and his real job as a heavy equipment operator for one of the new diamond mines. Trapping is now his hobby, his golf.

And I have visited with Larry Audlaluk of Grise Fiord, Nunavut, and listened to his story of how his family was forced to come to this place where they did not even know how to hunt the available animals, where the hardships were almost incomprehensible and where, over time, they stopped fretting over the past and came to love this stark place as home.

In my own career, I started out in magazine features and ended up a newspaper columnist, skipping altogether general assignment and beats and hard news. I sweat blood, I swear, when I have to do a simple news story, as happens from time to time.

The column is a very privileged position to work from. It can be what Teddy Roosevelt once called the presidency: "a bully pulpit." You can hammer; you can persuade; you can explain; you can deplore; once in a while you can even cheer. You can tell stories — my preferred style — or you can talk about yourself.

My colleague Jeffrey Simpson deplores what he calls "me-me-me" journalism above all else. My friend Charlie Gordon, himself a considerable columnist with *Maclean's* and the *Ottawa Citizen*, says you can use the first-person pronoun exactly three times a year — any more and you pay a penalty, sort of like exceeding the salary cap. Me, I like to think the column dictates its usage. If you're involved, you can be there.

But it is a slippery field. There is always the chance that in becoming so involved with yourself that you reach that point of no return once described by Chicago newspaper columnist Bob Greene in *Esquire* magazine:

"I fear I have lost the ability to live my life if it's not going to end up on paper.

"You could call that a classic case of workaholism, but I think it's even worse than that; I think I have lost the ability to live my life if it's not going to end up on paper. In a weird way, the putting of my experiences on paper has become the justification for having the experiences. If I'm not going to write about it, then I tend not to do it."

Scary stuff, that.

The thing is that yourself is the easiest and handiest topic. Requires no interviews, no fact checking, and often no travel.

A column is bloody hard work. Allan Fotheringham said, "writing a column is like making love to a nymphomaniac. You're no sooner finished work than you have to start all over again." John Ibbitson claims I said this to him when he first became a columnist. I don't remember it, but I'll take it: "A columnist is the only person in the world who wakes up each morning hoping someone he knows has died during the night."

Several years ago, the University of Ottawa hosted a symposium on the works of Morley Callaghan. I went along to listen to Leon Edel, a Canadian who went on to become the great Henry James scholar. He was then at the University of Hawaii and had some thoughts to offer on Callaghan's early work in journalism before he switched, full-time, to fiction writing.

"Journalists," Edel said, "live vicariously in a dubious half-world while believing themselves to be at the centre of things.... Some find it adequate for life; others find its bottomless superficiality and remove themselves to greener pastures."

I must say, I took that personally. I know of no greener pasture than journalism when it actually does something significant. Would we know about the sponsorship scandal without Daniel Leblanc's work at the *Globe and Mail*? Would we know about Maher Arar? Would there ever have been a second look at the Air India terrorist attack? Would Joe Volpe be future leader of the Liberal Party of Canada?

But journalism can still do a lot better in this country.

We are stuck with a mindset that Ottawa still matters as much as perhaps it did in the days when those who run the main media ships in this country passed through town. It doesn't. The Ottawa of 2006 and 2007 is not the Ottawa of 1966 or 1977 or even 1998. It has become, largely, an ATM where the premiers get to fight over the PIN.

The Hill is as over-covered as the National Hockey League is over-coached. The consequence of all this is that news is so thin in Ottawa, with so many good and competent reporters trying to justify their salaries, let alone their existence, that they will do whatever it takes to be noticed, to get their names out there.

There are, essentially, only two ways to break through this fog in Ottawa, and that is either to break real news — which most assuredly does happen from time to time, though not often — or else through pure mischief.

Mischief will get you on the front and high up in the news just as surely as will a great news break, so mischief, because of so much concentration on Ottawa, becomes a key player. Did the PM pay for his Grey Cup tickets? Who took the most government flights? Did the Governor General jump the queue to get her pacemaker? What exactly did Peter MacKay say?

Did Dalton Camp use his political connections to get a new heart?

How we wish that heart was still beating.

There is, of course, much to be said for having a strong journalistic presence in Ottawa. But there is also much to be said for having a much stronger journalistic presence elsewhere. Alberta, for example, is far more important these days than Ottawa is, and the North may soon become most important of all.

Had more journalists gotten outside the capital in recent years, they would have seen the gun legislation issue coming long, long before it became a financial issue. They might have learned that such "hot button" issues as same-sex legislation are hot only so long as there are journalists out there pushing the buttons. Don't push it, and Canadians don't even think about it.

My own out-of-town education happened several years ago when a man named Billy Diamond showed up at my National Press Building office with nothing more than a single sheet containing a news release from the Department of Indian Affairs. He said he'd been to the television networks and they had listened to him but decided against doing a story. Too far away. Too expensive. Too long to tell in a quick hit. I could, I suppose, have written a piece from Ottawa, with an interview — perhaps even a headshot — of Billy Diamond. But to *Maclean's* magazine's great credit, the magazine let me North to see for myself.

I like to think it changed my life.

I went north, by jet, bush plane, boat, at one point even rented a helicopter at $582 an hour and didn't first clear it with my editor. No phone — how could I?

I spent a long time with the Crees. I heard Billy Diamond's own story, the little kid born on the trap line, a yappy kid so smart his father, Malcolm, then the chief of Rupert House, sent him away to residential school so he'd have someone who could speak the languages of government for him.

I heard how Billy Diamond returned from high school with a tiny transistor radio. He came back hoping to talk his father into letting him go on to law school. But instead he was out on the spring goose hunt with his father, listening to the CBC news on that little radio, when word came that the province of Quebec was about to build the "project of the century."

They would build a hydroelectric project so large it would, like the Panama Canal, be visible from outer space. They would do this by damming the rivers flowing into James Bay and flooding the land — land the Crees had lived on and trapped on for ten thousand years.

And no one had even bothered to tell the Crees.

The story of the Crees' fight against this project is for another time. I think I have a book, on it somewhere; check the remaindered bins. That story is about the Crees' battle against two levels of government and huge multinational corporations.

To have some sense of what these sixty-five hundred Crees were up against, I will mention just the very first meeting young Billy Diamond organized in the village of Mistassini. The Crees had never had an official meeting of their leaders in all those ten thousand years. Some came by floatplane. Some canoed. Some even walked.

Billy Diamond had maps laid out in the little schoolhouse and started to explain how they'd have to set up an office to fight this battle when one of the leaders puts up his hand. "First thing we have to do is buy an electric typewriter," the man said.

Billy was confused. "Why electric?"

"Why electric? Because none of us know how to type — that's why."

From this starting point, the Crees managed a landmark court case and the landmark James Bay Agreement that gave them the first native self-government. It gave them money for economic development. It gave them their own schools — no more residential schools — and it changed the dams and rebuilt the villages and even moved one of the villages.

But the story Billy Diamond had come to Ottawa to tell, if anyone would listen, was not about government press releases. It was about dead babies.

The James Bay Agreement had broken down. The province of Quebec and the federal government had been ordered to work together to implement the agreement and one of the promises had been new housing and proper waste systems. One level of government would build the houses, another level of government would put in the sewers.

The houses were built — strong new homes that could survive that harsh climate — and the sewers were ready to go in. The ditches had been dug, the pipes and pumps were on order. But then Quebec and Ottawa got in one of their royal spats over some imagined slight and the project was put on hold. The Crees were forced to build outhouses in the backyards of those brand-new houses. In the spring, the sludge from those outhouses melted and drained down into the ditches. The ditches drained down into the water table, and ultimately into the well water.

The Crees had television reception now. The women, like women throughout the Third World, had been convinced, through advertising, that the modern way to raise a child was with formula. They bought formula from the Hudson's Bay store. They mixed it with the water from the wells. The babies got sick. They could not keep liquids down or in. Liquids poured out at both ends.

Little Tommy Wapachee of Nemaska was first to die. He was four months old. Soon there were others. Five more babies were dead. Some of the little bodies were taken away for autopsies and, the Crees said, one had been returned to the family for burial in a green garbage bag.

Philip Diamond, the youngest of Billy and Elizabeth Diamond's children, also fell ill. The baby was rushed by air ambulance to the children's hospital in Montreal, where the diagnosis confirmed the obvious: E. coli, gastroenteritis infection, the Third World killer.

It took a long time to get this story. *Maclean's* did it right, sending up photographer Brian Willer to go around James Bay with me and giving it full front-cover treatment. They never said a word when the bill came in for the helicopter. The story proved a great embarrassment to governments of Canada and Quebec. The Crees took the cover story and had it read into the record and tabled at the World Health Organization in Geneva.

One night, not long after the story appeared, Grand Chief Billy Diamond of the Crees of James Bay telephoned my home in Ottawa. Little Philip, he was happy to say, was recovering quite well. The federal cabinet had just met and earmarked sixty million dollars in emergency funds to repair the water supply. Our short conversation has never left me:

"Congratulations," I said.

"No," Billy said. "Congratulations to you. No story, and nothing would have been done."

Remember what June Callwood said right here four years ago?

"Journalism stands at the heart of democracy."

It's not a half world, Professor Edel, it's a whole world.

And, to my mind, there is no greener pasture to work in.

November 8, 2006

CHANTAL HÉBERT
The Changing Canadian Landscape

In the fall of 2007, Toronto Star *columnist Chantal Hébert came from Montreal thinking about new politics in Quebec from the perspective of one who spent a career writing about sovereignty: "What if you spent the best part of your life living next to a mountain only to wake up one morning to find it gone?" She is a guest columnist for* L'Actualité *and a weekly participant on the political panel "At Issue" on CBC's* The National *as well as Radio-Canada's* Les Coulisses du pouvoir. *She has served as parliamentary bureau chief for* Le Devoir *and* La Presse. *She knows that to understand Canada we must tell the story of Quebec. No one tells that story more coherently than Hébert.*

For most of the past half-century, the debate over Quebec's political future has been the defining feature of the Canadian political landscape. Love it or hate it, the presence of that debate has shaped the political perspectives of most of the people in this room for all of their adult lives — this speaker included. Every prime minister from Lester B. Pearson on down has been defined by his success or failure on what eventually came to be known as the unity front.

Aspiring prime ministers have been elected or defeated on the basis of their capacity to make an impression on Quebec. Robert Stanfield, Joe Clark, John Turner, Kim Campbell, and Preston Manning all failed in Quebec (and sometimes elsewhere) and all either failed to capture power or else failed to be confirmed in the post of prime minister.

Over time Quebec's presence has brought about a redefinition of the essential attributes required to aspire to national leadership. Canadian voters have come to reject the notion that one could seriously aspire to federal leadership without a demonstrated capacity to function comfortably in both French and English and win support in Quebec.

Political aspirants have responded accordingly. For the first time ever, a francophone federal leader — Stéphane Dion — is actually less bilingual than his anglophone competition — both within and outside his party. And a Quebec leader — Pauline Marois — is less bilingual than any of the three Ontario party leaders.

While that poses a problem for the Liberals and Dion and to a lesser degree to Marois, it is also a measure of the progress of bilingualism over the past four decades.

It was against the backdrop of the Quebec mountain that Pierre Trudeau brought Canada around to official bilingualism and eventually to the patriation of the Constitution and the Charter of Rights and Freedoms.

Brian Mulroney would not have achieved free trade without massive Quebec support. And that support would not have been so generously extended to a pet project of the business community had it not been for the efforts of Quebec's chattering class to make the province less dependent on the Canadian federation.

Jean Chrétien's landmark decision to stay out of the Iraq war was influenced in no small part by the strong feelings of his home province.

For better or for worse, Quebec and its existential debate has shaped Canada in ways that extend far beyond the realm of language and culture.

Now Quebec's tectonic plates are shifting. In what may be their most significant movement since the Quiet Revolution and the advent of the sovereignty movement, Quebecers are breaking out of the box of federalism and sovereignty.

For many Canadians who live outside Quebec, this is a startling change — akin to having lived next to a mountain for all of their lives only to wake up one morning and find that it is no longer there. The first reaction is often, and quite naturally, disbelief, a sense that some optical illusion is at play.

But if there is an optical illusion at play, it involves the enforced myopia of a great section of the Canadian political class that would not see peace in its time even if struck by it in the face.

For decades, leading Quebec sovereigntists and a strong section of the Canadian chattering class have shared a common misconception: and it is that the march to sovereignty is inexorable, or at least that it is unless every manifestation of Quebec nationalism is checked and countered. There has also been a widespread presumption that there were not within Quebec itself counter-mechanisms to keep the debate within the confines of a rights-oriented inclusive society.

Thus, to most Canadians outside Quebec, the debate about sovereignty has been about the breakup of their country. Their part in the discussion has largely focused on finding ways to advert it.

From that angle, accommodation, constitutional or otherwise, was framed in the context of setting back sovereignty rather than strengthening ties between Quebec and the rest of Canada. Federalism was presented to Quebecers as a comfortable default option to sovereignty rather than as a preferable endgame.

But what if those many Canadians — along with the sovereigntist elite — had been keeping score on the wrong battle? What if the board on which they assumed they were playing chess was really meant for a more simple game of checkers?

If there is one common thread to the past forty years of Quebec-Canada history, it is not the quest by Quebecers of their independence but rather the drive for political arrangements that are respectful — both of their identity and their collective capacity to ensure it within a democratic and inclusive framework.

Throughout that period, the preference of a critical mass of Quebecers has always been a federalist solution. Sovereignty, from its beginning, has been a default option to federalism, not the reverse. If there has been anything inexorable about the Quebec debate, it has been the prevalence of that federalist preference.

The Quebec sovereignty movement started to live on borrowed time right after the 1980 referendum — which it lost 60 to 40, where both camps currently stand. The circumstances of the patriation of the Constitution in 1982 — and Quebec's ultimate self-exclusion from the process — gave the movement oxygen.

Ultimately though, it was the constitutional crisis brought about by the failure of the Meech Lake Accord in 1990 that gave it a new and unexpected lease on life. Without the strong backlash unleashed by the Meech failure, the 1995 referendum would not have come about.

Just prior to the crisis, sovereignty was in decline. Many of its most talented promoters were re-engaging in federal affairs. In 1980 both Jean Charest and Lucien Bouchard voted yes to sovereignty-association. Within the next decade they were sitting side by side within the federal cabinet.

Perhaps the surest sign that sovereignty was on a slippery slope to nowhere was the massive Quebec support for the ultimately modest federalist Meech package.

But even the momentum of the storm generated by the constitutional debate could not carry sovereignty over the top. The bottom line is that for a majority of Quebecers, including many who voted yes, sovereignty remained a default option that they were not keen to exercise. Since coming so close in 1995, there has never been a time when sovereigntists could presume that they had a reasonable chance of winning a referendum.

That is not the result of a poor strategy on their part or a winning one on the part of federalist champions (who managed to misfire more often than they scored hits) — just think of the sponsorship mess, the Liberal civil war, the failure of the right to get its act together — but rather a reflection of a deep and contrary tide in Quebec public opinion.

The PQ tried to ignore it. It blamed successive leaders for its failure to move sovereignty forward. It insisted that once the natural tide of electoral politics brought it back to power, it would have a referendum, even if a majority did not want one. These days, it is finding sudden virtues in identity politics.

Liberal federalist champions, both in Ottawa and Quebec City, coasted on their credentials, assuming that in the face of a referendum threat, they would benefit from the fact that they were the only federalist game in town.

Both were swept aside by voters.

Last spring, the Parti Québécois scored its worst election finish in three decades, finishing third behind the Quebec Liberals and the surging Action démocratique. Pauline Marois is the first leader of the Parti Québécois who is not selected for her capacity to bring about a winning referendum.

Under her leadership, the PQ has put plans for a referendum on the backburner. Over the next year or so, she will be concentrating on modernizing her party's social democratic credo and trying to find a place in the debate over Quebec identity, in the absence of a game plan to take the province out of Canada. The first will ultimately be easier than the second.

At the same time, support for the federal Bloc Québécois has been eroding. That erosion was actually delayed by the sponsorship scandal. Prior to that story breaking out, polls showed that Quebec voters were poised to desert the Bloc en masse to support Paul Martin.

The federal Liberals are in worse shape in francophone Quebec than their Quebec cousins who can still claim some roots in francophone Quebec. The Conservatives and the NDP are making inroads at their expense and that of the Bloc.

Ironically, but not surprisingly, the only people — besides diehard sovereignists — who have been able to put a positive spin for sovereignty on these events have been diehard out-of-province federalists.

They have seen the advent of the ADQ, at the expense of the PQ and the Liberals, as a symptom of a federalist disengagement rather than a half-way house designed to break the sovereignty-versus-federalism cycle and the erosion of the right flank of the sovereignist coalition.

They saw a surge in Conservative support as a new immoral flirt between a federal party and separatist voters — as if Canada would be more sturdy if the one in two Quebecers who voted yes in 1995 did not participate in its national politics.

They saw support for the recognition that Quebec is a nation as the prelude to the dismantling of Canada rather than a symbolic gesture designed to allow a normalization of Quebec's situation within the federation.

And they saw a controversial proposal by the PQ to create a language-based Quebec citizenship as the beginning of the assertion of a strong streak of ethnic nationalism rather than the sad beginning of the end of a party that has been relegated to third place in the National Assembly. (The focus of the coverage on the proposal usually eclipsed the fact that the plan was dismissed out of hand by every other Quebec party, denounced by the bulk of commentators, and criticised by no less than Bernard Landry.)

Interestingly, and despite predictions to the contrary, a year after the adoption of the nation resolution in the House of Commons, there is no evidence that it has created great expectations within the Quebec electorate. On the contrary, there probably has never been a time since the Quiet Revolution when Quebec has put so few specific demands on the rest of the federation.

Instead, there is a vigorous and not-always-helpful debate taking place over the notion of reasonable accommodation of minorities. It is that debate that the Parti Québécois has recently tried to piggyback in a rather clumsy effort to win back its recently lost francophone constituencies.

There is less that is distinctively Quebec-oriented to this discussion than first meets the eye, and it certainly does not stem from the debate over the Quebec nation. Debate over immigration and the ways to maintain a socially cohesive society are hardly exclusive to that province. Ontario had a version of it under the guise of a debate on religious school funding earlier this fall. Indeed it was the defining feature of its election campaign. Most of Western Europe is having debates over integration and immigration these days, and they don' t always make for pleasant watching.

In Quebec as in Ontario, the focus of the discussion has almost exclusively been on religious accommodation. The decision to take religion classes out of the Quebec school system has routinely been described by a number of vocal groups as an affront to the culture of Quebecers, an attempt to water down their collective identity to unduly accommodate outsiders. Ironically, that decision was taken by a Parti Québécois government so as to reorganize the school system along language lines.

Another feature was an unhealthy, almost hysterical, focus on Muslims. That was a byproduct of the events of 9/11, the blanket coverage of previously marginal issues that has resulted from it, and finally the Canadian fighting role in Afghanistan.

All of the above are frankly twice removed from the concept of the Quebec nation.

The most significant fault line in the debate over reasonable accommodation, according to polls, is urban-versus-less urban and young-versus-old, with most people thirty five years old and under having no problems with the concept of reasonable accommodation and certainly seeing no threat in it.

Language, despite the best recent efforts of the Parti Québécois, and to a lesser degree the Bloc, has not emerged as a lightning rod. The reasons for that have to do with why the mountain of sovereignty has eroded.

There are many reasons why the sovereignist vehicles for Quebec nationalism are rusting, but the top one is language — or to be more precise, languages.

Most Quebecers no longer see sovereignty as essential to the preservation of a French-language society in North America. The texture of Quebec society has changed.

The Quebec language legislation has ensured that a much more significant proportion of newcomers to the province integrate into French. The so-called children of Bill 101, as they are called in Quebec, have in turn changed the social fabric of Quebec.

For two decades, Quebec has tilted its immigration towards francophone applicants and been relatively successful at increasing the French-speaking component in the mix of newcomers it allows in.

But it should be noted that the Muslim presence that is making so many Quebecers uncomfortable — including some who have actually never run across a Muslim Quebecer — is massively francophone.

At the same time, English is no longer seen as the language of a dominant Canadian class. Through globalization and the Internet, it has emerged as the lingua franca of a new globalized world. In the past, young French Canadians learned English, often under duress, as a condition to succeed in their own province and in Canada. They needed it to level the playing field. Today, bilingualism is an economic asset rather than just a historical necessity. Many Quebec francophones increasingly master it as a way to bypass Canada on the way to a larger stage.

In an era when national governments no longer exert the influence that they once had, arrangements with Canada are no longer seen as fundamental to the survival of the French language in Quebec. As a result, the Quebec-Canada debate is no longer the priority that it was for previous generations of Quebecers. The issues that mobilize Quebecers these days are global in nature: the environment and the war in Iraq, and to a lesser degree the fate of the deployment in Afghanistan and the impact of immigration.

Those who look to the debate over spending power or even the nation resolution for triggers of a new cycle of sovereigntist momentum are fighting the last war. Only under a radical change of paradigm and under different terms of engagement could the drive to Quebec independence find a second life.

The Iraq debate that saw francophone, allophone, and anglophone Quebecers march together in a mega-demonstration in the winter of 2003 probably contained more seeds of increased Quebec-Canada alienation than any debate on internal arrangements. But the merits of the contribution of a sovereign Quebec to the emerging debates are also less obvious.

A sovereign Quebec might not have gone to Iraq but it would have found it uncomfortable, to say the least, to be the only pocket of resistance to the U.S. bid in the upper section of the continent. A sovereign Quebec might do more to fight global warming but it would have less influence on the efforts of its Canadian neighbour. And as Gilles Duceppe has stated, it would have sent a contingent in Afghanistan as part of the NATO efforts in that country.

Finally, even on language-related issues such as cultural diversity, leading powers such as France for instance would rather have Canada — as a larger unit with links to the English-speaking world — in its camp against the Americans than just the small fraction of it that is Quebec.

The sovereigntist and federalist camps were, by definition, consensual coalitions. One was a sovereigntist or a federalist before one was a conservative or a progressive. The disappearance of the mountain is allowing those ideological differences to resurface. That, in turn, has profound impact on the federal scene.

The first casualties are yesterday's unity warriors. The Bloc Québécois is losing its appeal. It is undergoing a major crisis of relevance as Quebecers look elsewhere for vehicles for their new priorities. The federal Liberals can no longer command support on the sheer basis that they are federalist champions. They have become Canada's version of Cold War warriors. Now that the wall is coming down, their Quebec references come across as jaded and needlessly outdated. They are not so much rejected as considered irrelevant. That is costing them their title of natural governing party. The Conservatives and the NDP are tapping into pools of voters that they were at a loss to access only a decade ago.

Greater Quebec input within those parties will in turn transform them. Some of those changes are already noticeable in the Conservative party. In time if the federal NDP manages to build on its recent success in Outremont, it too will be transformed.

All of those are positive developments, but the alternative is unfolding in Belgium. This past summer and fall, Belgium didn't have a functioning government. In a country that has splintered politically along language and regional fault lines, even a common ideology no longer acts as a bridge between the Flemish and the French communities. As a result the winners in Belgium's national election were unable to craft a working coalition, and there was a possibility that the country would implode.

There were those who argued that the fracture may have been helped along by proportional representation. But, as the 1993 election demonstrated with the advent of the Bloc Québécois and the Reform Party, our first-past-the-poll system is no guarantee that regional interests will not trump national institutions.

But if the electoral system is no insurance against fragmentation, a strong national political culture is.

In contrast with Canada, where basic minority language rights are guaranteed by the Constitution and extend from coast to coast, Belgium has taken a territorial approach to language, with regions outside of the capital operating solely in the language of the majority.

At a time when the Bloc has arguably never had as much influence, with successive minority governments in place, Quebecers are turning to larger national coalitions on the right and the left — coalitions that are led by politicians who do not hail from the province and within which the Quebec contingent will automatically be outnumbered.

A decade ago, a critical mass of voters in the rest of Canada refused the invitation to support a party, such as the Reform, that was marketing itself as the voice of Canada without Quebec. Today, the failure of Stéphane Dion to engage his own province is what stands to ultimately damn him in other markets.

From the angle of the post-unity era, the most important Canadian story of this political decade is not whether Stephen Harper does manage to turn his Conservatives into the natural governing party. Nor is it whether the NDP overtakes the Liberals as the top progressive voice in the House of Commons or, eventually, that both may be forced to consider a merger rather than give the right a quasi-permanent lease on power as the result of division on the left.

These are compelling stories, with much significance for future fundamental debates. But the more compelling one is the rebuilding on the right and on the left of Canadian political coalitions that allow Quebecers and other Canadians to cohabit under the same roof and come together around common goals without leaving who they are at the door.

Keeping Quebec in the federation has been the dominating challenge of the second half of the twentieth century in Canadian politics. But living productively with Quebec may be one of the transforming experiences of the first Canadian decades of the twenty-first.

November 7, 2007

KEN WHYTE

Be Interesting, or Else

A decade after he gave Canadian journalism a kick in the backside as the founding editor of Conrad Black's brash National Post *newspaper, Ken Whyte came to campus. Most recently, as editor of* Maclean's *magazine, he had been reviving the tired newsweekly and would soon be named president of Rogers Publishing. During more than two decades in the journalism business in Canada, Whyte was called many things, but boring wasn't one of them. He is a senior fellow at Massey College, University of Toronto, a governor of the Donner Canada Foundation, and a director of the Peter Munk Public Policy Foundation. He is also the author of a biography of William Randolph Hearst, a man who also understood that there's no point to this enterprise if nobody's reading.*

I confess I was a bit surprised that I was asked to give this lecture. I accepted as soon as I was invited. But I wondered if the organizers really knew what they were getting by inviting me. As you know, this event has been going on for six years, which makes me the sixth journalist to deliver the lecture. And to be honest I don't think I would have made Dalton Camp's list of six favourite journalists. In fact I'm pretty sure I would have made his list of six least-favourite journalists.

I was editor of the *National Post* when it launched in 1998 and Mr. Camp at that time was a columnist for the *Toronto Star*. He was a good columnist. I don't want to slight him in any way but I think it's fair to say in 1998 that he was still best-known as an author of books and as a

Conservative Party insider and commentator on Peter Gzowski's CBC show. He'd been writing columns here and there, including in the Saint John *Telegraph-Journal,* but in my opinion he was considered a political guy who wrote a column, rather than a real live journalist. He held his own on the page, but even his publisher at the time, John Honderich at the *Toronto Star,* acknowledged to me that Dalton Camp had yet to hit his stride as a columnist, and that changed after the arrival of the *Post.*

The *Post,* at the time, was a paper of many enthusiasms and first among them was its self-assigned project to build a viable opposition to the ruling Liberals, who, in the wake of the implosion of the Mulroney Conservatives looked like they'd run Canada forever. What used to be the Conservative Party had fractured into the Reform party, the Bloc Québécois, and a Tory rump overseen by Joe Clark. The *Post* was cheerleading for a merger between the Reform Party and the Tories — that whole Canadian Alliance episode — and we weren't especially patient with Joe Clark who was reluctant to play along. Dalton Camp, for his part, wasn't especially patient with us. He was a supporter of Mr. Clark and he thought the whole unite-the-right project was nuts. He'd given his life to the Tory party and he wasn't about to see it overrun by what he considered a bunch of rednecks and neocons with bad ideas and worse manners. He came to life as a columnist in response to this threat to his Conservative Party and the *Post* became his favourite punching bag. Hardly a week went by when we weren't the target of his derision and his towering outrage. He called the newspaper dishonest, an abomination. He called our esteemed proprietor Conrad Black a pompous, vindictive, spiteful reprobate. He also called him an unregenerate thief, which was unfair — at the time.

To give Mr. Camp his due, he did from time to time give the *Post* some backhanded compliments. He said that our competitive efforts had made his morning paper, the *Globe and Mail,* a better paper. He considered the *Globe* a grey, garrulously vapid, and politically backward newspaper and that was the single point of agreement between Dalton, Conrad, and myself. Anyway, after a few years of this back and forth between our paper and Mr. Camp I ran into the *Star*'s John Honderich and he was ecstatic about the performance of his columnist. "It's like Dalton's been reborn," he said. "And it's all thanks to you guys." And Honderich was right. Dalton Camp in those years was a superb columnist and it was an honour to be mercilessly attacked by him in the *Toronto Star*, Canada's largest circulating daily, week after week after week.

Which brings me back to my original concern about whether I'm the right person to be delivering this lecture. I don't worry about that anymore. Dalton Camp flourished as a journalist in response to the *Post*. I was a major contributor to his growth and his achievement as a columnist so I've earned this honour. Come to think of it, I should have been asked a lot sooner than sixth.

I never had the pleasure of meeting Mr. Camp but there's no doubt he was a fine Canadian and a distinguished public servant and a political force and an unfailingly interesting journalist. And interesting journalism is what I hope to talk about tonight.

I was asked a couple of months ago by Philip Lee what I wanted to discuss in the field of journalism and I told him I'd review my own experiences as a journalist. I'm going to talk about my long history of work at profitless publications. It's a sad story, really. My first job of any consequence was at *Alberta Report*, a weekly newsmagazine that was a shoestring operation that survived by selling subscriptions to people who wanted an alternative voice to the leading dailies in the province — the *Calgary Herald* and the *Edmonton Journal*. Those dailies were polite, somewhat dull, probably too liberal for the sensibilities of their audiences but they were rich with advertising. *Alberta Report* was boisterous, combative, conservative, and poor. It had next to no advertising but it did survive for many years on the strength of its voice. It knew that it had to be interesting every week or that it would go out of business. I was the executive editor of the magazine during what I naturally consider to be its heyday in the mid 1980s. We ran the circulation up to new highs and we won magazine of the year honours at the Western Magazine Awards and we lost a lot of money, consistently, sometimes prodigiously. And never a year went by that we didn't read rumours in the newspaper of our imminent demise.

After *Alberta Report* I became editor-in-chief of the venerable Canadian monthly *Saturday Night*. That was an entirely different publication. It had exquisite taste and high literary standards and I found myself editing the likes of Mordecai Richler and Alice Munro. But my experience at the magazine really wasn't a lot different than my experience of *Alberta Report*. We had very good circulation, we won quite a few awards, and we posted losses every year that I worked there, and we regularly read reports in the newspapers that we were about to be shut down. I should add in my own defence that these losses in both cases started long before I got there.

After *Saturday Night* I was named founding editor of Canada's newest national newspaper, the *National Post*. The trick at the *Post* was to convince people who already had a newspaper that they needed another one, which meant we had to be really, really interesting or we were going to go out of business. Beginning with a circulation of ninety thousand, the *Post* climbed in two years to a circulation of about three hundred thousand. The *Financial Post* called us the most successful broadsheet newspaper launch in the English-speaking world in fifty years. The paper's losses ran to a spectacular nine figures and I was dismissed by the new owners in 2003. Rumours of the *Post's* demise were heard even before it published its first edition and hardly a month went by all that time that we didn't read that the whole thing was about to come crashing down and we'd be out of work and those rumours, of course, persist to this very day.

In sum, in each of the twenty consecutive years that I served at *Alberta Report*, *Saturday Night*, and the *National Post* I read at least one media report of my money-losing publication's imminent collapse. I did so without ever experiencing that collapse and claim that as a record unprecedented in the history of print journalism. I'm not sure if that's true but I claim it.

I was going to talk about that tonight because I've long been aware that my experience in journalism hasn't been run-of-the-mill. Most other people I know in the business have worked at big, stable organizations, mostly daily newspapers that have quasi-monopolies in their markets.

They attract a lot of advertising and they return solid profits. I've worked, until recently, only at precarious publications that existed because their owners thought their journalism was worthwhile and they were willing to put up with their losses. The publications were kept in business because they had something interesting to say and because readers wanted them. They were reader-driven rather than advertising-driven and I wanted to talk about the difference between those two models and how it shapes your values as a journalist.

That was my plan last summer, but a lot has changed in the meantime. As of today, I'm no longer really unique in my experience of working for money-losing publications. Now it seems everybody I know in the business is working for a money-loser. The industry's a mess and I'm fast becoming a cliché. So while I'm going to make some points, still, about the difference between reader-driven and advertising-driven journalism, I'm going to do it in the context of these momentous trends in our industry, instead of in my own, small career.

The really bad news in the industry, this wave of it anyway, started last October when the *Christian Science Monitor,* in its hundredth year of publication, announced it was ceasing to exist as a daily newspaper and would henceforth be published online. In its last year it had revenues of just over $12 million and expenses of $31 million for a $19 million loss. About six weeks after that the Tribune group, which publishes the *Los Angeles Times* and the *Chicago Tribune* — the *Chicago Tribune* that spent most of the twentieth-century boasting of itself as the world's greatest newspaper — filed for bankruptcy protection. It was losing $124 million a quarter. It had debts of $13 billion against assets of $7 billion. No sooner had that news landed, than the *Seattle Post-Intelligencer* and Denver's *Rocky Mountain News* were both put up for sale and threatened with closure. The owners of the *Star Tribune* in Minneapolis sought bankruptcy protection. The *Atlanta Journal Constitution* was reported to be losing a million dollars a week and in danger of closing. The *Detroit Free Press* cut its home delivery schedule to three days a week as a cost savings. Just days ago, Gannett, owner of *USA Today* and many other large American papers, announced it was requiring employees to start taking weeks off, unpaid. Even the mighty *New York Times* has been hit. It began selling assets at fire sale prices just weeks ago including a share of its own head-quarters and sold some of its equities to a Mexican communications king, Carlos Slim. Closer to home, the *London Free Press* and the *Kingston Whig-Standard* are among the papers who have already cut print days or are planning to do so in the near future. The *Globe and Mail* just an-nounced massive layoffs in response to catastrophic declines in advertis-ing, as did the CanWest newspaper chain. The *National Post* is no longer available in huge parts of the country. *Time* Canada, my chief competitor at *Maclean's*, announced several weeks ago that it was closing its doors.

Thousands upon thousands of jobs have been lost in print in the last few months. Advertising bookings continue to dry up. Newspapers that once reliably posted returns of twenty to thirty percent a year, some of the most reliable returns in all industry, are now deep in the red. It's the worst catastrophe in print journalism since the Depression and it may be worse than what we experienced in the 1930s because nobody then believed that newspapers were likely disappearing and many industry watchers now believe that printed dailies will cease to exist in the not-too-distant future.

As I mentioned, I'm no stranger to operating losses and threats of closure. I can usually just shrug them off and move on, but what's happening now does have me concerned and I've given some thought to what's happening and what it means. The easy answer for what's happening is that the Internet has stolen readers and advertising, particularly classified and real estate advertising, from newspapers, and that these trends combined with a severe economic slowdown are killing the newspaper business. Newspapers are vulnerable to the Internet because the Internet can deliver the same information faster and cheaper than old-school publishing with its dead trees, and expensive presses, and door-to-door delivery. I think that's about half the story. As for what it means, the common answer especially among newspaper people is that the decline of newspapers will damage our public sphere, and sap the vitality of civic discourse, and undermine democracy. Who, if not the daily press, will bring us accurate and reliable information from town councils, from Ottawa, from Kandahar? Who will champion the vulnerable and expose corruption in high office? We can't trust all that to bloggers. I think those concerns are almost entirely misplaced.

I take the long view of these issues. What's happening to the press and what it means in the long view where newspapers are concerned is really long — about two hundred and fifty years since Benjamin Franklin published what's generally considered to be the first daily newspaper in North America in Philadelphia. And if you look across that span of time, I think it's pretty clear that newspapers have been on the decline not just for the last few months, not just for the last few years, but really for about a hundred years, since the early twentieth century. I acknowledge that the twentieth century was good to some newspaper owners, and that individual journalists and newspapers did some exceptional work in that time. But I think the newspaper business, as a whole, has been fat, lazy, and arrogant over most of the last hundred years and that it has also undermined journalism and democracy in important ways. We should recognize that before we worry too much about what's happening to the industry today.

The newspaper world we've known since the early twentieth century has a lot of shortcomings and they can be seen most clearly from the vantage point of what came before, mainly the newspaper world of the nineteenth century. I want to give you a brief overview of those times and our point of contact with them will be William Randolph Hearst, who coincidentally is the subject of my new book, *The Uncrowned King*. You probably know William Randolph Hearst by reputation. He was one of most powerful and fascinating citizens in twentieth-century America. He had an enormous chain of newspapers and magazines, a radio network, a motion picture studio, the country's most spectacular private residence — a 71,000-square-foot hilltop castle at San Simeon — and perhaps, most famously, he was identified as the model for Charles Foster Kane in Orson Welles' classic *Citizen Kane*. Back in 1895, W.R., as he was known to his colleagues, was a relative unknown. In fact, both of his parents were more famous than he was. He was the only son of George Hearst, a wealthy U.S. senator, and Phoebe Apperson Hearst, Washington's leading socialite and a great American philanthropist. Young W.R., a Harvard dropout, was a tall man, broad in the chest, somewhat gangly with large feet and hands, and he tended to fidget. He had a long face, piercing blue eyes set close together; he had pale cheeks, light brown hair, and a voice that was said to bleat thinly like a toy flute.

He also had a genius for newspapers. He'd already enjoyed some success as owner of the *San Francisco Examiner*, but he knew that to really make his mark in publishing, he needed a triumph in New York, which was already the media capital of the world. So, using family money he bought a struggling newspaper in New York, the *New York Journal*, and sought to become a player on that scene. It was a very crowded scene in 1895. There were three million souls in New York when Hearst hit town. It was a diverse metropolitan population. It was already the city that never sleeps thanks to a huge volume of traffic, tramcars, omnibuses, and elevated trains. The population itself was noisy, it was restless, and it was hungry for news. We like to think we live in a media-savvy age and we tend to think back on the nineteenth century as the dark ages of journalism, but there were forty-eight newspapers in New York when Hearst hit town — thirty-six of them in the morning and twelve in the afternoon. Most of these papers sold on the street for two or three cents a day and these pennies comprised the bulk of a publisher's income. Obviously, the bigger your audience the more money you made and some of them became very rich. It was a very competitive newspaper market and papers worked hard to distinguish themselves from their rivals by identifying with particular classes or political interests. All papers tended to be noisy about their own politics and unfair and unbalanced about everyone else's. There were highbrow newspapers, lowbrow newspapers, trade union papers, commercial papers, gossip sheets, and foreign-language newspapers. There was a paper for every taste and every point of view. Not only did the city support all these papers, but many of the papers routinely produced three or four editions a day and as many as twenty or thirty editions when the news got hot. This gave rise to a 24-7 news environment long before the phrase ever occurred to us.

The newspaper-reading public was discriminating. An abundance of choice makes smart, demanding readers and they shifted around to whatever paper was doing best at the moment. A bright new paper, one championing a popular cause, one with the sharpest feature writers, one with the most scoops, could double its circulation inside of a year. A failing paper could fall just as quickly. The tendency of readers to move around from paper to paper made the distinctiveness and the excellence of a daily's content matter in a way long since lost to journalism. As a result, it mattered whether or not a newspaper had top journalistic talent. Editors with a gift for divining the priorities and the interests of their audiences were in high demand and paid like bankers. I can assure you that's no longer the case, although in recent months the gap has apparently closed.

Writers and artists who not only had something to say but who could be heard above the crowd were courted and poached from paper to paper and they were paid as lavishly as television talent is in our time, the Jon Stewarts and Jerry Seinfelds of the world. That the whole business revolved around readers — attracting readers, holding readers — fostered a respect for public opinion among all classes of journalists. Editors believed it was their job not to preach to people, not to tell them what to think, not to study them at arm's length, but to speak the sentiment of the people. There was very little cynicism at the time about public opinion. This was partly because it was a more democratic age and partly because one's financial success depended upon one's ability to keep faith with one's audience. If an editor ceased to reflect the sentiments of his readers, if he ceased to fight hard for their notions of liberty and justice and democracy, if he ceased to deliver the enterprising journalism and the moral leadership that the readers expected he'd fall from public favour and his business would suffer. At that time it really was be interesting, or else.

There were problems with this approach to journalism. The clamour for public attention among the newspapers was noisy and sometimes very messy. Demagoguery was a constant temptation, but readers weren't stupid and they weren't gullible, and editors knowing the ups and downs of public favour cared for their reputations and they held themselves to recognized standards and they mercilessly policed each other and pointed out one another's errors and failings. It wasn't neat and it wasn't tidy but a healthy democracy seldom is.

At the very top of the heap at this time in New York was Joseph Pulitzer, a native of Hungary who made it big in America by building one of the first great mass-market newspapers. He had an unerring instinct for the big story. He developed a dramatic style of news presentation with big headlines, illustrations, and cartoons, and he adopted a friend-of-the-people political style that went over really well with working-class New Yorkers. Pulitzer had a circulation of around 250,000 a day and one of the largest incomes in America as a result. Just a few years before Hearst's arrival, Pulitzer had built a monument to his own success, the Pulitzer building. It was sixteen storeys high, 309 feet, the tallest building in New York, the tallest building in America, and the tallest commercial structure anywhere in the world. It was a monument not only to Pulitzer's success, but to the power of mass media, mass-market daily newspapers, which were the first mass medium.

I can't emphasize enough just what a big deal newspapers were at this time. We take them for granted now, but back then they were bigger, fresher, more fascinating than Microsoft or Google are in our time. They were globe spanning, multimillion-dollar businesses. They were among the most complex organizations then known to man. They employed heroic amounts of labour, material, and capital. They recruited the best managerial talent and invested in the latest, most sophisticated technology. They used the telegraph, the telephone, and magnificent printing presses that ran a mile a minute. They had armies of reporters, bright, ambitious, college educated men who scoured the globe for the latest news and information. It was widely believed that newspapers then possessed a collective genius not exceeded in any other branch of human effort. Given how small government was at the time newspapers were often better informed on far-flung events than elected leaders. They exerted real influence. A big newspaper's support could swing a presidential nomination for a single candidate.

Newspapers could do this because they spoke to an audience on a given day bigger than the total sum of audiences that the presidential candidate would speak to in an entire campaign. This is of course in a pre-broadcast age. People spoke then of the newspaper age with the same enthusiasm and awe that, when I was a child, people spoke of the space age, and people now speak of the digital age. Charles Dana was one of the great editors of the nineteenth century. He used to say, "what a wonder, what a marvel it is that here, for one or two cents a day, you buy a history of the entire globe from the day before. It's something that is miraculous, really, when you consider it. All brought here and printed. All brought here by electricity, by means of the telegraph so that the man who has knowledge enough to read can tell what was done yesterday in France, in Turkey or in Persia. That is a wonderful thing." And it was at the time an entirely new thing.

Hearst, on arriving in New York, immediately set his sights on Joseph Pulitzer. He wanted to be top of the publishing heap. He started with a circulation of fifty thousand. He imported his best staff from San Francisco and hired some of the best people in New York and he turned his *New York Journal* around in a matter of weeks. He doubled his circulation in a few months and he caught Pulitzer after about one year. After three years he was himself the leading publisher in America and his New York paper became the cornerstone of the largest publishing empire the country had ever seen. It would be said at one point in the early twentieth century that one in every four Americans was getting his news from a Hearst paper. Just how he did this is the subject of *The Uncrowned King*.

The conventional take on how Hearst triumphed in New York is that he produced a single-minded, simple-minded paper catering to the lowest common denominator, to recent immigrants and the marginally literate, that he filled his paper with society gossip, crime and scandal, big slashing headlines and melodramatic storytelling, that he wallowed in sensationalism and lurid journalistic excess. I found looking into it at length that that judgment of Hearst's work relied almost entirely on the testimony of Hearst's publishing rivals and his political enemies of which he had many. Anyone who's spent any time in media or in politics knows that probably the least reliable statements you'll ever hear are when media and political types talk about their competitors. That was the case then, as well.

Looking at the contents, the actual contents of Hearst's newspaper and his rivals, paying particular attention to the records of the impartial observers around at the time and there were many, I found that Hearst had in fact succeeded by putting out the best and most popular newspaper in the city. He had the best stories, he had the best columnists, he had the funniest cartoons, he got the biggest scoops. He had the most colourful and fascinating feature stories and the most exciting interviews. He held to a radically progressive politics that appealed to a broad base of working-class New Yorkers and his politics sharply differentiated his paper from everyone else in town. He did a lot of what all newspapers are supposed to do — tell the truth and shame the devil, expose corruption and injustice — and he did it better than anyone else in New York. He was able to build, almost overnight, a publishing franchise with eventually a million readers in a savvy newspaper town because he was a brilliant editor and because he spoke the sentiment of a large segment of the public. He didn't race to the bottom. On the contrary, he improved the quality of all newspapers in the market. His *New York Journal* was a demanding and sophisticated read for the time and it makes most of our dailies today look dull and tongue-tied. This runs counter, of course, to the conventional view of Hearst, but it makes sense that he would have had to produce a good newspaper if he was going to succeed in New York, given the variety of papers there and the savvy newspaper reading public.

My point here isn't to burnish Hearst's legend but to point out some of the dynamics of the nineteenth-century newspaper world: that readers mattered, that newspapers competed for their attention, and that a paper like Hearst's, a new paper with pluck and intelligence and talent and a fresh political outlook could find a big audience almost overnight. Publishers were constantly innovating and chasing the best journalists to please their readers. Readers could find themselves reflected in the newspapers they read. There was always at least one newspaper in town speaking to their priorities, to their politics, to their tastes. This made people feel a part of civic discourse, a part of their communities as though they had a stake and a voice in things. It's not entirely a coincidence that the highest level of voter turnout in American history occurred in the midst of this vital and highly competitive world of nineteeth-century publishing.

Even as Hearst was making his reputation in New York, the reader-driven business model that he had mastered was dying. Advertising was becoming a big business in the nineteenth century and just around the time Hearst triumphed in New York advertising revenue passed circulation revenue — money from readers — to become the lion's share of a publisher's income. A few years later, in 1905, advertising revenue had grown to be fifty-seven percent of a publisher's income, and by 1914 it had rocketed to two thirds of a publisher's income. It would soon after reach fourth-fifths of a publisher's income. It stayed there for most of the twentieth century and remains there now.

This flood of advertising completely changed the game. A publisher's job was no longer to get the most readers, it was to get the most advertising. That's a different business because advertisers and readers want different things. Readers want newspapers to tell them what they want to know, to speak their sentiments, and to fight their battles. Advertisers want a safe and sedate print environment for their ads. Henceforth, the ability to deliver a sedate and safe advertising environment was more crucial to a daily's financial success then its ability to speak the sentiments of its people. That is a fundamental and consequential change.

It changed journalistic values. Journalistic values are not etched in stone; they tend to change with business models. In the new world of an advertising-driven press, newspapers lowered their voices and brought in their elbows. The aggressive, politically charged audience-building tactics of the great warrior editors like Hearst and Pulitzer gave way to the relatively bland consensual habits of business managers who wanted only a minimum of readers necessary to keep their advertisers happy. Papers relied less on their ability to move the hearts and minds of ordinary people and more on their utilitarian, non-controversial attractions — the basic feed of objective information — sports scores, weather reports, classified ads. The new papers made virtues of their detachment, their impartiality, and their moderation.

Editors from the previous century would have considered these new publishers to be eunuchs in the public sphere because they rarely went out on a limb, they rarely took a hard stand or fought for their readers but advertisers loved the news guys and they all got rich. At least, those publishers that were still around got rich. The predominance of the advertiser in the newspaper world encouraged a massive wave of consolidation in the first decades of the twentieth century. Big publishers began buying little publishers and cities that had once supported a dozen or more papers were left with three or two or one newspaper. The number of dailies on the continent has been falling since 1915. Advertisers were perfectly happy with this and encouraged it because it was cost effective to reach a whole reading public in a city by placing one ad in a paper rather than a dozen. Publishers liked it, or at least the big publishers who survived, because they'd learned from oil refiner John D. Rockefeller and other monopolists around that life was easier without competition.

The absence of competition made increasingly bland newspapers blander still. When you're alone in a market and you need to satisfy a whole city of readers rather than a particular class or political constituency you naturally hug the middle. You strive for consensus, for inoffensiveness. You favour balance over the assertion of truth and you wind up lying like a wet blanket over the city that you're supposed to cover. The absence of competition also made the development and promotion of newspaper talent more or less unnecessary. Why pay writers or artists big sums of money when you're the only employer of newspaper talent in town? Where else are they going to go? And what difference does it make if your best columnist runs off to write a sitcom? You just replace him with someone else who may only be fit to write death notices, but you're not going to lose any readers because you're the only source of news and information in town. People are reading you because they want the news, they want sports scores, they want weather reports and grocery prices — they have to take you.

As a result of all this remuneration in the newspaper business slid in the twentieth century and the best and brightest people did move on to other mediums and into other fields. By the end of the century the talent pool was so shallow that people like me could make a pretty good living at it. Worst of all, the absence of competition allowed newspapers to stop innovating to please readers. Monopolists have little incentive to ever change their ways. It doesn't matter if you're giving readers the same old routine, that your funnies aren't funny anymore and haven't been since the 1940s. Readers have nowhere else to go.

Hearst and Pulitzer between them either invented or brought to a higher stage of development almost all of the features that we like in newspapers today, everything from sports sections to lifestyle or women's sections, op-ed sections, signature columnists, illustrated weekend sections, colour comics, flexible typography, photo illustration, photojournalism, humour sections, games, puzzles, unprecedented civic activism, and spectacular crusades. The twentieth century inherited all this but added almost nothing of its own. Its principal contribution to the development of newspapers was the advertising environment — all those food and travel and auto sections. That's a very small contribution frankly, a pathetic contribution, for a whole century of newspapering.

I'm not alone in my opinion of these trends. In fact, going way back to 1925, the great American editor William Allen White said that his once lively and noble profession had been transformed into nothing more than a profit-taking scheme, a reliable eight percent security. His only mistake in that is that the security became even more reliable in the range of about twenty to thirty percent through most of the century. The media critic Michael Wolfe meant much the same thing just a few years ago when he said newspapers had become, like the people who run them, faceless, personality-less, reliable, bureaucratic. All that can be said for them is that the businesses throw off tons of free cash flow. Wolfe calls it the public utility age of newspapers. Reporters, he says, once clever and disreputable, became something like public service employees. The institutional blandness that overtook newspapers helped turn them into a medium for old people.

Now I would admit there were good things that happened in twentieth-century newspapers. Some dailies became more reliable. Some became more polished. Many of the newspapers that did survive and get very rich could afford to invest in journalism, and did invest in journalism, and produced some outstanding work. But at the same time there's no escaping the fact that the twentieth-century business model, the advertising-driven model, brought the expansive, innovative, competitive world of nineteenth-century publishing to a close, and that the press has never been as diverse and as enterprising as it once had been, nor as responsive to its readers. It now spoke, and has spoken for the last hundred years, with less eloquence and has fought with less conviction. It has no incentive to do otherwise. I should add that voter turnout, a key measure of the health of a democracy, swooned throughout the twentieth century in North America.

Now we're in the Internet age, the Internet is in full bloom and all those utilitarian elements of newspapers that publishers counted on in the last century to hold their audience — basic news feed, sports scores, and want ads — they're all easily available, at no cost, online. And advertisers are moving online as well. Newspapers have to make new arguments for their relevance, especially to readers, and they're struggling to do that. They're not used to thinking hard about readers.

Those are some of the reasons that newspapers are in decline now and have been, I think, for the last hundred years. I don't want to be unsympathetic to people in the business today. I feel for the individual papers now threatened with closure and for the many journalists who've lost their jobs, but I do believe this reckoning is necessary. I think newspapers, if they are to survive, have to adjust. They'll have to reconsider their methods from top to bottom, and they'll have to rediscover how to make themselves interesting and relevant to readers in an exceedingly competitive journalistic marketplace. I'm optimistic many papers will survive and they'll do this. They'll find different priorities and different business models and they will adjust.

Meanwhile, I don't think we should waste any time worrying about our civic dialogue in the absence of healthy newspapers or the newspapers we're accustomed to. The forces at play in publishing today are likely to produce a livelier and more diverse public conversation and a much healthier democracy. The Internet will be good for journalism in the long run, I think, because it operates in a ninteenth-century manner. It's all about attracting eyeballs, about pleasing readers, about speaking to be heard above the crowd, about the competition of ideas and methods, styles and tastes. It's about being interesting. Advertising is a source of income on the web but attracting readers is the key to getting advertising and thus the key to success. The online business models need a lot of working out. There's nobody who's perfected them yet but that will come. And in the meantime, I note that voter turnout in the United States, after falling throughout the twentieth century, has, in the last decade, the first decade of the Internet, begun to climb again.

For the young journalists out there, aspiring journalists coming into the business, I don't think you'll have careers like most journalists had careers in the twentieth century with secure jobs at big rich metro papers or big rich networks, their departments, and their bureaus, and their many levels of management. I think your experiences will probably be a lot like my experiences: working for news outlets that exist primarily as vehicles for journalism, not as vehicles for advertising. They'll be there because you have something to say and an audience to say it to.

I think you'll spend a lot of time thinking about what readers want and what interests readers and why and that will convince readers to subscribe to your website or your publication as opposed to the other guy's. And I think that's a good thing. You'll be in the news business, not in the advertising business. Hopefully you'll get some advertising. Advertising's great so long as it's not driving the train and the businesses you work for will be more profitable than the ones I worked for. Either way, you'll be making a living by communicating with people and that's a wonderful thing to do. I'm sure that as soon as we get out of this awful recession there'll be a lot of great things awaiting you.

You have been a very attentive audience and I thank you very much.

Q: My name is Tim Andrew and I'm not sure if this is an entirely fair question. You haven't mentioned magazines. Do you see the same thing happening to magazines as happened to newspapers? They, after all, in many cases, are far more advertising-dependent than newspapers are.

A: I think the magazine industry is a lot more diverse than the newspaper industry. We have everything from *The Economist*, which I'm told is profitable on its circulation revenue alone, to women's magazines that are ninety to ninety-five percent driven by advertising. Some of them are undoubtedly going to have trouble. *Time* Canada, I mentioned, has shut down and *Time* U.S. is in just a horrible state right now. It's losing advertisers, losing readers. *Newsweek*, as well, *U.S. News* — most of our competitors in fact are really struggling. *Maclean's* has fifty percent of its revenue coming from readers and fifty percent from advertisers, which is a really nice balance, but if our advertising goes down twenty percent we're going to suffer along with everybody else. We do have, though, that safety net of our relationship with our readers and the willingness of our readers to pay for the product and I'm hoping that's going to give us some cushion. The magazine industry hasn't been hit, on the whole, as hard as newspapers but...well, let me make an exception to that. One part of the magazine industry that got absolutely killed by the Internet long before anyone else in publishing was really watching or really worried was the adult market. You used to go into a newsstand and a third of the shelves would be given over to adult magazines. They're almost all gone now and everything's on the Internet. Those were a lot of really big publications that got just smashed. *Playboy* was at one point the biggest magazine in America. It was a Fortune 500 company.

Q: My name is Russ Hunt and I've been concerned for a long time about the fate of journalism because it seems to me that journalists need to be paid, and the money needs to come from someplace, and when I look at the history of the Internet, the short history, I don't see where the money's coming from. It's easy to see that there's lots of people writing stuff and that there's lots of eyes looking at it and I can put my blog up and people will read it, but I don't know who's going to pay for it. The tradition of the Internet has been that you supply it for free or it dies and I don't see a structure whereby the important work of journalism that has to be supported by an institution is going to be continued in this situation. I guess I'm less optimistic than you are and maybe you can help me by suggesting where that money might come from.

A: A few points. First of all, I think one of the great things it has done is allow people to disseminate information themselves so a lot of functions of journalists are being taken over by amateurs and enthusiasts. They're seeking out documents, they're seeking out information, and they're distributing it to people who want to know about it. Often a lot of important issues have big life on the Internet before they ever hit the mainstream press.

And I agree it's nice for journalists to be paid. I like to be paid. But it's not really necessary that we get paid a lot and in fact through most of history we've been badly paid except for that time I was talking about in the late nineteenth century. Through the seventeenth and eighteenth centuries and most of the nineteenth century it didn't pay much at all. Now, I think, because you've got so many people participating in our civic conversations and I think because a lot of them on these websites and on blogs will eventually find ways to make some money that will sustain them — they already are — I think the need for paid journalists is a lot less than it has been before.

Take that one step further. I think it would be great if we could still have institutions of journalism that are able to afford journalists who do more investigative work, more detailed work, more comprehensive work, and if there's a public demand for it I think they'll still be able to operate. I think newspapers are going to struggle, they're going to be restructured, they're probably going to be smaller, but they'll still be around and they'll still be able to do a lot of their essential functions. So the paid journalism jobs aren't going to go away forever and some of these websites are going to get really big and really successful and they'll be able to attract advertising. Already they're starting to support journalists. For one example, you see what's happening in the sports world right now, these big sites like ESPN, Fox Sports, and some of the others are starting to hire some of the better talent away from magazines like *Sports Illustrated* and use them exclusively online and they're paying them very, very well, and they get enough advertising online to sustain that. I think that will happen in other fields as well as people learn how to talk to audiences online and how to develop their journalism and package their content. We're in a time of flux right now and it's going to take a while for the old business models to reconstruct and new business models to emerge, but I think it will happen.

January 28, 2009

SUE GARDNER
The Changing Media Landscape

This talk was a homecoming of sorts for Sue Gardner, who began her career at CBC Radio in Fredericton before becoming one of the world's most influential media figures. When she arrived on campus in the fall of 2009, she was the executive director of the Wikimedia Foundation, a collaborative Internet project that revolutionized the sharing of information, including news. Before joining Wikimedia, Gardner spent a decade as a reporter and producer for CBC Radio, eventually guiding the development of the CBC's online news services. In the spring of 2014, she left Wikimedia to devote her time to other projects, particularly those related to maintaining an open and free Internet. In a rapidly changing media world, Sue Gardner never stands still.

We hear a lot these days about the crisis in journalism. News organizations everywhere are shrinking; they're laying off staff. Newspapers are shutting down. Public broadcasters around the world are struggling to justify their funding. The old business models are crumbling, and new ones haven't yet arisen to take their place. There is a lot of concern.

What I want to do today is reflect on some of the changes that are taking place.

If you take one thing away from my talk, I would like it to be a renewed sense of optimism. I believe we're currently experiencing a golden age. There is more information — more breadth and depth and quality — available to people today — easily, for free, from anywhere — than has ever been the case in human history.

I think we're all a little confused about what's going on, and we're missing the real story.

The traditional media has an enormous megaphone, and it is emoting anxiety. That makes sense: the future of traditional news media is murky and fraught with challenge.

But that needs to be separated from our own story. We — news audiences, news consumers — shouldn't let ourselves be distracted by the problems that are being experienced by the journalism industry. What we are experiencing is good, not bad.

I thought I would start with a very simple example.

Twenty years ago, I lived here, in Fredericton, New Brunswick. My first job as a journalist was working as the associate producer on the CBC Radio afternoon show.

Here's what my media diet was back then in 1990: I read the *Daily Gleaner* and the Saint John *Telegraph-Journal*: the two local papers. I got a slimmed-down "national edition" of the *Globe and Mail* — and it was pretty slim. I listened to CBC Radio compulsively. I subscribed to the *New Yorker* and *Harper's Magazine*, both of which were very expensive for Canadians because they cost a lot to ship. Sometimes on Sunday, I would go down to a little coffee shop on Regent Street and pick up the *New York Times*. Those were all relatively mainstream media products.

But I also had some interests that were slightly less mainstream. I cared about alternative music, and I cared about film. So I subscribed to what used to be called "fanzines" — tiny photocopied magazines about alternative culture. They were labours of love, written by amateurs, typed up and photocopied and mailed out by hand to a few dozen or a few hundred subscribers. They were hard to find, and most weren't very good, but I subscribed to them because they were my only real connection to that stuff. They weren't mass products.

That was my media diet in 1990.

Today, I read many, many, many more newspapers and magazines, but I read them all online for free. My old, unsatisfying diet of bad photocopied fanzines has been replaced by a multitude of options for specialized information. I have access to hundreds of excellent blogs and sites covering economics, politics, fashion, restaurants, real estate, law — every topic imaginable. Wikipedia exists now. As does Google News, Twitter, Salon, Slate, Wonkette, Politico. And on and on and on.

Just twenty years ago, getting information was hard. It was expensive. And as an information consumer in 1990, not all my needs were met. The economics were such that media needed to be designed for a mass audience. If you weren't a mass audience — if you cared about alternative music, if you were a Canadian outside Canada, if you had minority tastes of any kind — you could not get what you wanted. The costs of production were just too high to serve small groups of people. For the most part, niche audiences got lost.

What's been happening in the past twenty or so years, is that some of the costs of production have evaporated. That's why we have an explosion of options, because news and information are cheaper to create now than ever before.

Physical materials, paper and ink, are expensive. You don't need paper and ink to publish online. Distribution, the cost of trucks and drivers, satellite towers, cable, that was also expensive. Today, Internet infrastructure is cheap and getting cheaper.

The last major cost for news media has been labour: researchers, reporters, editors, photographers, managers. In some of the new models, but not all, that work is done for free by amateurs. Increasingly, people prefer to consume news and information online; that's what all the studies show.

This leaves traditional media companies with a huge problem. They still need to pay all the old, high costs of traditional news production: the trucks, the satellites, and the staff. Beginning in the mid-1990s, they also needed to start investing online, so that they'd have a foothold when online audiences started to grow. So their costs are increasing. Meanwhile, the old forms of subsidy, display advertising, classified advertising, even government dollars, are increasingly going elsewhere and bypassing traditional media entirely. The local car dealership used to advertise in the local paper: now, some of that money goes elsewhere — like to the dealership's own website or to Google AdWords. Nobody pays for classified ads anymore; they go to Craigslist. The Canadian government builds its own Canadian culture sites, instead of handing that money in trust to the CBC. So the traditional media organizations were in a bad place, with rising costs and declining revenues.

And then we had the global economic crisis, last year, which sucked even more ad dollars out of traditional media. That's when we saw newspapers in particular begin to really collapse. They had not made enough headway online to secure a future there, and their old world had crumbled into dust around them.

So: we're in the middle of a hugely disruptive period. Nobody knows what will work. My old friend Robert Harris tells me it's a little like the early days of radio. To musicians, it was obvious that radio stations should pay them to play their music — because they made it, and the radio station was going to make money from it. To the radio stations, it was equally obvious that the musicians should pay, because being on the radio would make the musicians famous, which meant they would sell more records.

That's essentially what's happening today in the news industry. Some news publishers hate Google News: they say Google is stealing their audiences by publishing, under fair use, snippets of their stories. Other news publishers are grateful to Google for pointing people towards them, and optimize their pages to get a good Google News ranking. Should Google News pay Rupert Murdoch, or should Rupert Murdoch pay Google News? Or should nobody pay anybody? Nobody knows.

I think that over time, the business models will shake out. If enough people use a product or a service and they like it, ultimately their use will generate enough money to keep the product or service alive. It may turn out to be a subscription model or pay-per-use or advertising or philanthropy — but money will find a way to reach producers, if the product is useful. That mixed-funding economy will shake out over the next ten years or twenty years, and it will continue to evolve and iterate after that. It's not clear what it will look like, but what is clear is that we're in the middle of a very disruptive period, where there will be lots of experimentation and very little clarity. But in the end, people will find ways to ensure they get the stuff they want.

At Wikipedia, we are right now in the middle of our annual fundraising campaign. Our premise is simple: you use Wikipedia. Three hundred and thirty million people around the world use Wikipedia every month. You use Wikipedia, so you should give a small donation to keep it going. That's our basic message. And it works. People love Wikipedia — it is always there when they need it, and our experience is that they are therefore willing to pony up some small amount of money to keep it available for themselves and for others. It's a similar model to what NPR does. And it works.

I'm actually not that interested in business models: that side of things will work itself out. If people like stuff, they will find a way to keep it available. What I find more interesting is the story from the audience perspective, so that's what I will talk about here today.

I'm going to tell you why this is a golden age for information, and I'm going to challenge some of the common objections to this new world, that I think just aren't true.

There are three main reasons why this is a golden age of information: quantity, freedom from censorship, and convenience.

The first reason this is a golden age is that the quantity of information available to average people today is higher than ever before in human history. The perfect example of that is Wikipedia.

Wikipedia has fourteen million articles, which makes it about two hundred and fifteen times as big as the *Encyclopaedia Britannica*. That means it's got room for all kinds of mildly obscure information. Wikipedians — who are all volunteers — sometimes jokingly call Wikipedia the world's largest and most authoritative compendium of information about Pokémon. Transportation enthusiasts have lovingly developed articles about the world's highways and railway stations and subway systems. Kids and civic-minded people everywhere carefully polish articles about their schools and their towns.

Most of that would never warrant inclusion in *Britannica*. But that doesn't mean it's not useful. We know that somebody somewhere wants that information, or else the Wikipedia articles would never have been written. Wikipedia gets 330 million visitors from around the world every single month. People want this information.

Wikipedia is the largest collection of knowledge ever assembled anywhere. You could not have created Wikipedia in the old world, if you'd needed to pay for paper and trucks and writers. But Wikipedia's editorial staff works for free, and the costs of bandwidth and servers are tiny compared with the old costs of printing and shipping. In a world of cheap, perfect digital copies, Wikipedia, and countless other information publishers, thrive, which is good for people like you.

That's the first reason we should be happy — there is more information available to us today than ever before.

The second reason to be happy is freedom from censorship. It is very hard to impede the free flow of information online. There's a famous quote from Stewart Brand who said, "information wants to be free" — and it does. We see it again and again: people will use whatever tools they have to share news with each other. And the Internet makes that much easier than ever before.

We saw this most recently, and famously, during the protests surrounding the Iranian election last June. The aftermath of the election included lots of direct attempts to censor people's access to news, by directly intimidating and harassing journalists, filtering and shutting down websites, blocking satellite signals, and so forth. But a very interesting story that emerged was how Iranian protestors successfully used Twitter to share information with each other and with the rest of the world.

Now, it's obvious that all the information put out via Twitter was not necessarily accurate — it was just ordinary people doing it, after all. So they might have been wrong, or confused about what they saw, or they might have repeated wild rumours. Journalists do some of that too, but ordinary people are probably likelier to do it. It's also true that tools like Twitter are vulnerable to exploitation: for example, a government worker could pose as a protestor and send out misinformation. That is also less likely to happen via professional media.

But even having said all that, the net result of Twitter use during the protests following the Iranian election was a benefit. People inside Iran and outside it had a better understanding of what was going on than they would have otherwise.

Twitter was so useful that the American State Department officially asked it to delay an upgrade, because that upgrade would have made Twitter unavailable for the Iranian protestors during this key period. The State Department thought Twitter was too important to be offline, for even a few hours.

What's great about that is that technologies like Twitter are hard to censor, because they are tools that lots of people use. Ethan Zuckerman, a fellow at MIT's Berkman Institute, calls this the "Cute Cat Theory." If millions of ordinary people use Flickr and YouTube and Twitter to share pictures and videos of their cats, and talk about how cute their cats are, but meanwhile, a few activists use those same tools to share information, that makes censorship very difficult. If you block Flickr, huge numbers of people freak out because they want to share pictures of their cats. Those cat lovers provide cover for tools that are also used for more important purposes, such as sharing information that would otherwise get suppressed.

We've seen it again and again. It has become commonplace: people using tools like SMS and Twitter and Wikipedia and Facebook to share information that governments or corporations or other interest groups do not want them to have. That's a good thing.

This will sound anticlimactic, but the third reason we're in a golden age is convenience.

Convenience is a funny word — it's a marketing term that exudes cheapness. It has a yellow, house-brand aura to it. But convenience is actually really powerful and important, because people are really lazy. If I have to set the PVR, I might not bother. If I don't have the right change, or I'd need to wait eight weeks for delivery, or would need to go to the faraway store, not the store that's close — people are lazy.

I am a pretty motivated information consumer. But even so: when I lived in Fredericton back in the early nineties, there were many, many weeks in which I was insufficiently motivated to walk to the corner store for the *New York Times*. I knew less stuff because I couldn't be bothered to walk a half a kilometre. Imagine that, but multiplied a million times.

Convenience really, really matters. Today, we can get news and information from anywhere in the world, on any topic, with no planning required, for free, right now. That's powerful.

It's a golden age, because there's more information available than ever before, it's less censored than ever before, and it's ridiculously cheap and easy to get.

I want to address some frequent criticisms of the digital world:

The most common objection is quality-related, that Wikipedia and other sites like it just can't be trusted. I also often hear that people feel deluged by information; there is just too much available. And then there's another very serious criticism: that the Internet creates a kind of echo chamber, where people only hear their own voices reflected back to them.

The first objection people raise is quality. And I'm afraid Wikipedia — the site I work for — is often Exhibit A for why this is not a golden age, but rather an illusion, a house of cards. People say it to me all the time: "anyone can edit Wikipedia. I think my neighbour's kid edits Wikipedia. Surely it is full of mistakes and nonsense."

Depending on the context, there are a couple of answers I might give. If I don't know the person well, I would tell the person that actually, every study — and there have been many — concludes that, in fact, Wikipedia contains roughly as many errors on a per-article basis as any other major encyclopedia, such as the *Encyclopaedia Britannica* or the German encyclopedia *Brockhaus*. It's true: I can point you to the studies. I would admit Wikipedia is vulnerable to vandalism, but about half of all vandalism is reverted immediately, and most of the remainder gets cleaned up within a few days or weeks. Part of the strength of Wikipedia is its ability to self-correct — print media is notorious for taking forever to publish retractions or clarifications or updates; online media can fix mistakes immediately.

But if I were talking to a friend and she said, "surely Wikipedia has mistakes in it," I might be tempted just to laugh and say yes. Because so does the *New York Times*. And so does CNN. And so does the BBC.

For a long time, we all suspended disbelief and believed in authority. If you had a beautiful authoritative voice and projected an aura of reassurance we believed you. We chose to believe that quality news institutions did not make mistakes. That was wrong.

Today though, we're all going to get the credibility we deserve. Some blogs are credible, some are not. Most conventional news operations reach a minimum standard of credibility, but some don't. Individual Twitter accounts have varying levels of credibility. It will take a while for all that to shake out. But I think once we get through it, and we've developed new norms and signifiers for trustworthiness, we'll be further ahead than ever before. The real story isn't that some information shouldn't be trusted — that has always been true. The real story is that trust should be earned; it shouldn't be granted easily. We used to grant it too easily. We all need to get good at parsing out what is trustworthy and what is not.

The second objection I hear a lot is that there is simply too much information for any one human to make sense of. That it is too hard to navigate the morass of stuff available. We are deluged with information, and it's impossible to parse out what's important, and what isn't.

The best answer to this I have heard comes from the brilliant New York University professor Clay Shirky. Clay reframes the question — he says the problem isn't information overload: it's filter failure.

This is related to the economics of publishing. When publishing was expensive, the onus was on publishers to enforce quality. If people would definitely be interested in something, publishers would publish it. If it were unlikely to interest many people, they wouldn't. They couldn't afford the financial risk. It was their job to ensure that quality and relevance was high enough to interest people.

But if the upside of limitless space online and low production costs is a wealth of information, the downside is that we now must apply a quality filter. We can have anything, and therefore we have the problem of having to sort through it ourselves.

I think that's a problem that's going to go away. Where there's an itch, people will find a way to get it scratched. Informational filters are already being developed to help us. Spam filters are screening out email that nobody wants to see. Online forums sometimes filter comments based on commenters' reputations, screening out comments from people who are not generally considered to be adding much to the conversation. RSS readers allow us to privilege sites we think are good.

I believe that over time we will develop better and better filters to screen out stuff we don't care about. I also believe that we, as people, will adjust. We'll get used to the idea that there's more available to us than we can possibly ever consume. This is a good problem to have. And we'll adapt.

The final myth I'd like to challenge is the one about self-reinforcement. Many people feel the Internet will serve to reinforce a tendency people have to surround themselves with people like us. That fragmentation and self-selection will subdivide into little tiny echo chambers, in which we only hear from people like ourselves, and our views are never challenged.

There's a really interesting American book called *The Big Sort*, which suggests this is happening in the real world, offline. Increasingly, the book shows, people are selecting into geographic communities of people just like them — with shared demographics, attitudes, and political convictions. The author of the book did a photo-essay quiz for *Slate*, asking people to guess whether snapshots were taken in red states or blue states. It was easy to tell — in Berkeley, California, people are growing geraniums in their backyards in bathtubs, and in the deep south there are gun racks on trucks. You don't see bathtubs planted with flowers in rich suburbs of Dallas, and you don't see gun racks on trucks in Westchester County. It is true, and it is worrying, that people have such a strong desire to shut out different viewpoints, and to cluster so tightly with people who are just like them. It's a human truth.

The Internet is full of tiny echo chambers full of confirmation bias. I stumbled across a fashion site the other day that made me laugh out loud. It was a community of young women in highly conservative professions — like law and finance — who gathered together to discuss fashion.

Their topic areas: what precise features distinguish between a navy pump that is office-appropriate and a navy pump that is not; a skirt length that hits one inch above the middle of the kneecap — is that too short? What is better: a double strand of small cream pearls, or a single strand? I loved it; it was a hilarious echo chamber about appropriateness.

During the last American presidential election, my stepfather and I were talking about echo chambers. He had been spending time on sites populated by extremely fervent anti-Obama activists — the people called the "birthers" — you remember this story. They had been trying to claim Obama couldn't run for president, because he wasn't actually an American citizen. The claim was that he was born in Kenya, or possibly Indonesia, rather than in Honolulu. The Obama campaign had released his birth certificate but the conspiracy theories and lawsuits continued.

My stepfather had discovered online networks of these conspiracy theorists — who were full of rage and lies, and who were all seemingly reinforcing each other's worst tendencies. It was a big echo chamber of nonsense, and he was horrified by it; he had never really seen that level of vitriol and lack of respect for fact.

I think the real story there is not that the Internet enables conspiracy theorists to find each other and to self-organize and self-reinforce — although I believe that, to a degree, it does. I think the real story is that other people, through the Internet, can get a window onto those groups. We geographically, increasingly, self-select to be with people like ourselves. The Internet allows us to visit and experience people who aren't like us. I spent a ton of time during the last American election, reading very, very extremist political blogs. I would never have heard those voices before the Internet made them available to me, and I found them fascinating.

Sunlight is the best disinfectant. That means it's better for us as a society to have a window onto all the communities who are unlike ourselves. It's interesting to be an online tourist into other places, and it can help foster a better, deeper understanding of other people. That can't be bad; it can only be good.

I'd like to close with a little story. A few months ago, I was at the Aspen Institute — it's a think tank in Aspen, Colorado, which convenes small thoughtful conversations about pressing issues related to public policy.

I was part of a conversation about the future of media and how we could ensure people would, in future, continue to get the useful, high-quality information they need in order to make good decisions and support a strong functioning democracy.

There were about twenty of us there, people from the "disruptive" side of the equation — me, Craig Newmark from Craigslist, and Marissa Mayer from Google — but also people from the conventional media side of the equation — old-school publishers and journalists. It was a bringing-together of two worlds: the old world and the new.

There was a guy there named John Carroll who I found really interesting. He is an older guy who used to be, years ago, the executive editor of the *Los Angeles Times*. The *Los Angeles Times* has been having a lot of difficulty —like most newspapers — figuring out a business model that will work online. And they have found themselves faced with some pretty tough and uncomfortable choices, and they have made some decisions that made many people unhappy.

The most controversial: in April of last year, the *Times* ran an advertorial on its front page, promoting an NBC TV show called *Southland*. The advertorial was written like a news story, it looked like a news story, and it wasn't labelled as an advertisement. It has always been generally agreed in the journalism industry that advertorials are a bad thing, particularly if they're not labelled as such. And this wasn't. It was really not obvious the *Southland* story was advertising, and paid for by NBC.

There was a lot of protest inside the newsroom and from readers, and the paper later said it had made a horrible mistake. It also said that it needed to "innovate or perish," and that it needed the money.

At the Aspen conference, John Carroll characterized himself a number of times as a dinosaur from another era. He talked about the old media values of honesty and integrity, truth, fairness and neutrality, about serving the audience rather than serving advertisers. He said, in effect, that he has been getting increasingly sad and uncomfortable seeing the wall between advertising and editorial, which has long been in place and long been maintained, seeing it crumble in the face of difficult economic times. He was worried that the world is getting worse, and quality journalism getting harder to find.

While John was talking I was feeling this enormous sense of sympathy, because I believe in the old values too. That's why I went into journalism; it's why I spent seventeen years working for the CBC. I knew the *Times* story a little bit, and it has made me sad too.

But I think John's conclusion is wrong, and I told him why. The reason the news industry developed a wall between advertising and editorial was because there has always been a real danger of interference. I want to say honestly: all publishers pressure their editorial staff. They can't help it; it's built into the system. As a publisher, you need to make money, which means you're susceptible to pressure from whoever pays your bills. The high costs of production in the traditional media industry created that vulnerability, and that's why we needed a wall, and that's why the wall was always porous, aspirational rather than bulletproof. That's part of why, for example, journalists joined unions — to create an extra layer of protection against interference.

The attempts to protect newsrooms against inappropriate pressure are imperfect efforts to solve the real, existing problem that publishers interfere with journalists. It also means news audiences are less well-served.

It's true that the wall is getting more porous, not less, for traditional media organizations. Difficult financial circumstances have made them more vulnerable than they used to be. But the same isn't true of the new organizations, and that's the part I think John missed.

In effect, I am the publisher of Wikipedia. At Wikipedia, my costs are pretty low, which makes it easier for me to resist pressure. I might face uncomfortable choices, if my expenses were ten or one hundred times what they are. But even if I faced uncomfortable choices, at Wikipedia I have no ability to pressure the editorial people. They're volunteers. I don't pay their salaries. I don't control their career path. I have no ability to harm them, and I have no ability to offer them rewards. Many of them, I don't even know their real names, I will never meet them. They are not particularly accommodating: they are every bit as fiercely protective of their independence and their integrity as any journalist I know. They too have the old values — they want to serve the reader.

So people call me up all the time because they think that Wikipedia's article about them is broken, and they want to see it fixed. The first phone call I ever received at Wikipedia, in fact, was from the CBC's communications department, complaining to me that an article about a CBC sportscaster contained a serious inaccuracy.

In cases where an article is inaccurate or biased, I can turn the person over to a Wikipedia editor, and they will get it fixed. In the case of the CBC sportscaster, I did that, and seven minutes later, a Wikipedia editor I have never met and do not know corrected the article. Because Wikipedia editors are good people — they want Wikipedia to be accurate and neutral. In those instances, my intervention is not seen as inappropriate.

Often the person calling will want the article polished; they want to remove stuff from it that is true. For example, a company will want to remove information that doesn't reflect well on it, or a public relations person will want an article about their client to be more flattering. I'm happy to say that in those instances, there is absolutely nothing I can do for them. That's a good thing. Anonymity and decentralized production and production by volunteers makes information systems stronger, not weaker. It fixes an old brokenness that was bad for journalism.

I don't know if I persuaded John Carroll to be more optimistic. I think he understood that I'm on his side, and that I share his values. And I think he was pleased when I told him that Wikipedians admire people like him, and that they admire quality journalistic institutions.

Whether I persuaded John Carroll or not, it is clear to me: we live in a world where more people than ever before have easy, quick access to a huge quantity of relevant, high-quality, constantly updated information. We're in a disruptive period, and we can expect to see more media institutions crumble before this is over. But it's a golden age for information: it has never been better for people like me, and people like you.

November 18, 2009

STEPHANIE NOLEN

Shrapnel, Snakes, and Blistering Rage:
On the Occupational Hazards of a Foreign
Correspondent

Stephanie Nolen came in from the field with her five rules for success as a foreign correspondent. She's been doing that job and doing it well for two decades, filing memorable stories from South Asia, Africa, and the Middle East. She has won a record seven National Newspaper Awards for her reporting. Her book 28 Stories of AIDS in Africa *won the PEN "Courage" Prize and was nominated for the 2007 Governor General's Award for Non-Fiction. She is now the Latin America correspondent for the* Globe and Mail *and lives in Rio de Janeiro with her partner and two children.*

It's a huge honour to be part of a lecture series in Dalton Camp's memory. It was one of my great pleasures in life, as I'm sure it was many Canadians', to listen to Kierans, Lewis, and Camp on *Morningside* every Friday in the Gzowski years — although I had no idea then how hard it was to make good journalism look that easy.

The thing about journalism these days, of course, is that everybody's doing it. Everyone's got a blog and a podcast, and between Twitter and the iPhone video app, the citizen journalist is ubiquitous and increasingly influential. Major news organizations, including my own, seem convinced that this is the future of newsgathering, no doubt in part because it's much cheaper than the upkeep of an old-school foreign correspondent like me, but also it's sexier.

So, if I'm going to be put out of a job by a fourteen-year-old with a webcam and a blog, I figure the least I can do is try to make sure she is doing good journalism. I have been a reporter for twenty-five years, and a foreign correspondent for most of the past seventeen, and I thought that perhaps the most useful thing I could do for you this evening is offer a few tips , particularly for those of you who are journalism students — so herewith my five key rules for success as a correspondent:

Rule #1: Show Up

You may think that's a bit obvious. But two years ago — after I had a great many years in which to have learned better — I very nearly missed one of the most important stories I have ever covered because I almost didn't go. I was based then in the *Globe*'s Johannesburg bureau, and there was an election coming in Zimbabwe.

I had covered a great many elections in Zimbabwe by that point, and they all went the same way: the valiant opposition did the best they could, Robert Mugabe's henchmen beat them and jailed them and stuffed the ballot boxes and stole the election. Every time. And the Zimbabwean people sighed and dug in for a few more years of acute suffering.

It was a heartbreaking story to cover, painful not least in its sameness, and it came with an additional layer of danger, in that the Zimbabwean government would not allow foreign reporters into the country so one had to sneak in — my usual cover was "birdwatcher" — binoculars, bird book, big goofy hat. It was a fiction that would have held up for about three seconds under interrogation since I'd be hard pressed to identify a seagull, but a photographer friend had taught me to shriek, "Malachite kingfisher!" while pointing at a leafy tree: he said that would be very convincing. I used to do that periodically when I was sneaking around interviewing opposition activists who probably thought I was completely mental.

If caught — and I knew many reporters who were caught, since the government devoted considerable resources to keeping us from reporting on what it was doing — if caught one faced near-certain physical assault, and weeks or months in one of Zimbabwe's hideously overcrowded jails until your ambassador got you out. So this was a high-risk proposition. I had other big stories to cover that March, I had a young baby, and I thought — do I really need to go to Zimbabwe to watch this whole charade again? And risk time in Harare Central Prison? I could already write this story. We know what's going to happen.

But then, a couple days before the election, my fax machine began to whirr and it spit out a letter of accreditation, inexplicably provided to me by the Zimbabwean media commission. I will confess that my first reaction was, "*Damn.*" Because now of course, I had to go. I, Adrienne Arsenault from the CBC and her crew, and some Finnish journalist were the only reporters accredited for this election, something we never figured out. I thought: if I'm legal, I've got a moral obligation to go, because there are going to be no legal correspondents; I'll be able to openly interview people and this may be the only way the opposition can do public interviews, and now I have got to go. So I very reluctantly flew up to Harare and set out to cover another exercise in blatant voter intimidation and election rigging that would set Zimbabwe further along the path of its horrific decline and be largely ignored by the outside world.

But, of course, that wasn't at all what happened. The Mugabe machine did everything it could to steal that election, and it failed. Mugabe didn't win. And this incredibly brave network of Zimbabwean election monitors had the numbers to show it. They couldn't get that data into the Zimbabwean media, because Mugabe had killed, jailed, or exiled every independent journalist in the country. But they got the data to me, and to a colleague of mine from the *Washington Post* — I got it on the *Globe* website within hours of the vote — and then the genie was out of the bottle. There was no way for Mugabe to pretend that he'd won. He still managed to force a run-off vote, he sent his goons to beat and to rape and to burn the houses of thousands of opposition supporters, and he clung to the presidency — but he was forced into a power-sharing government with the opposition, and it was the beginning of the change. The election I came within hours of opting not to cover was the beginning of the end of one of Africa's last dictators. I came *that close* to not going. So rule one, show up.

As a footnote to this story, let me tell you that the dark irony is that despite my being accredited, I was arrested not once but twice in the course of covering the election. I was not held long either time, but they were not pleasant experiences. However, they did result in the Canadian ambassador in Harare using her diplomatic immunity to bring me my breast pump in prison — which is my personal favourite story of my tax dollars at work.

Rule #2: Go Where the Story Is, and Then Get in Deep

The more you read, the more people you talk to, the more questions you ask, and the more time you spend listening to the answers, the better the story you will write, record, and shoot. There is a direct proportional relationship between the amount you know about something and how good a story you tell about it — this is an immutable and unchanging rule of journalism. It's as true in the era of Twitter as it was back when correspondents rode into Afghanistan on horseback and spent three weeks with the mujahedeen, rode out again with their tapes in their saddlebags, and *then* put together their stories.

There's not a lot of patience in today's newsroom for that kind of reporting, but there is no substitute — absolutely none — for actually going to where a story is, for the simple reason that the story very often is not what you think it is before you get there.

There was this very sensational story in the newspapers not long after I moved to New Delhi about a "caste murder" — a young woman who was allegedly killed by her family because she had eloped with a guy from a lower caste. Caste discrimination of course is outlawed in India's constitution, and nevertheless goes on all the time. I thought this murder might be a good way to talk about some of the tension between the new India and the old — the young woman was a college student, her husband was an IT engineer in Delhi. They had very "New India" kind of lives, but they were caught up in thousands-of-years-old ideas. So I tracked down the young man and spent a day looking at his legal documents and talking to him. Something about it all seemed odd, so I called up some of the Indian reporters who had been covering this story, to ask them what the police had told them, and what they found in the village where the girl's abduction and murder by her family allegedly took place. And they all said, "Oh, I didn't talk to the police. We didn't go to the village." No one had been to the village — which was only two hours away in the next state.

I went. And the story I got from the police was quite different from what I'd been told so far. In the girl's village, the story was different again. It wasn't clear, in fact, that the girl was dead — the widely held view there was that in fact she'd been sent away to an auntie in a very rural area and was being held there. I couldn't ascertain the truth of that. But what became very clear, in talking to neighbours and friends and her teachers was that they didn't think of it as a caste murder. Her friends and teachers talked about this young woman, Monika, as a strong-willed and independent person with a vision of her life, living on her own in the city with a professional job, which clashed badly with the image held by her conservative family and in particular with her older brother. He who had appointed himself to the role of decision-maker for her life — or, I suppose, been appointed to that role by thousands of years of tradition and Indian culture. They fought and fought, I learned, and Monika ran away, and he dragged her back home and beat her up; she lied and snuck out and did everything she could to have the sort of life she wanted in the city. And if she was dead, it was because her brother had refused to tolerate further defiance, and had carried out his repeated threats to kill her.

This was also a disturbing story, of course, but it wasn't, particularly, a story of caste. Rather, this was a story about gender in the new India, about women and their place in a society that is rapidly changing — although not rapidly enough to help Monika. The caste story, the gender story, they're both important, but only one of them was accurate, was true, and that's always the one you want to tell.

A second footnote, and second dark irony: after I came back to Delhi and wrote about this, all of those Indian reporters called me up to do follow-up stories for their papers based on my reporting gleaned from me actually going there.

This rule is the underlying principle of the best journalism I have ever done. Two years ago I won a National Newspaper Award for a story about why child mortality was declining in the poorest countries in the world, down by as much as 30 percent. I saw that statistic in a press release and I wanted to know why, how that could possibly be? How is Niger cutting child mortality by 30 percent? Because there's nothing good happening in Niger; that, I mean, is the sad truth. In Malawi, there's not a lot of good, not a lot of growth, not a lot of progress coming from Malawi. Why are they cutting child mortality so dramatically?

And I phoned some experts who had some good-sounding theories. Then I went to rural Malawi, and I sat under trees, and I talked to a lot of mothers about why their babies weren't dying — which was one of the more pleasurable assignments I had in six years in Africa. The mothers didn't talk about new drugs and they didn't talk about health policy. The difference was that the government had taken about six thousand people with a grade four or five education and trained them as community health workers. They taught them how to give measles shots and encourage women to breastfeed, give vitamin A to six-month-old babies, a step that costs less than five cents and has a huge difference on immunity levels. The public health plan was using people who could barely read, but who had cut child mortality by 30 percent. The story I got from those mothers was the right story and it was also way more interesting.

This year I won a National Newspaper Award for a piece about why India continues to be home to half of the world's malnourished children, why the number of malnourished children has not changed at all despite nearly 10 percent economic growth per year for more than a decade. I heard that statistic at a press conference, and I wanted to know why — and I spent months talking to people about it, and I heard a lot of interesting theories, but then I went out to some villages in Madhya Pradesh, places where more than half the children are acutely malnourished. I spent a lot of time talking to families about, literally, what they ate for breakfast, and I discovered the answers I had heard so far were wrong. Many of the people formulating nutrition policy in the Indian government or for aid agencies, who perhaps coincidentally had never been to a village to talk about breakfast, were also wrong. The answer was that, in those villages and all over India, men decided what they planted, and what they sold, and what they cooked, and who ate it. Typically in those families, the women cooked seven chapattis for breakfast, and the father ate four and the sons ate two and the mother split the last one with her daughters. Women in Ethiopia or Liberia were, on paper, poorer, and lived in far poorer countries — but their children were healthier because those women could own land, could work it, cooked the food, and decided who ate it. The women fed their children, and they had much lower rates of malnutrition. A few days in villages made it very clear that the status — and lack thereof — of Indian women was the reason child nutrition was so critically poor. That was the truth. *And* it made a better story.

So, following those two examples, we come to rule number three.

Rule #3: Be a Woman

I had originally conceived of rule number three as Always Talk to Women — because as you may have gathered by now, it has been my experience that the information you get from women makes for the most compelling and the most illustrative stories.

I am asked all the time if being a woman makes my job harder. People often seem surprised when I say that not only does it not make it harder, it makes it so much easier, to the point that I can't imagine doing my job, actually, if I weren't a woman. The reality is, that between religious prohibitions and cultural ones, if you're not a woman, you can't talk to women in about two-thirds of the world. You simply don't have access.

When I was in Pakistan last spring to cover the government's war on the Taliban, I did many of the same sorts of stories that my male colleagues were doing — about the greatest displacement of people in South Asia since the partition of India in 1947; about the dire humanitarian conditions in which these two million refugees were living, about the lack of an effective humanitarian aid response; about the on-again, off-again military strategy the government was employing against the Islamists, about the connections of this conflict with Afghanistan.

But I also did another story, and I was the only reporter to do this story. It was about how the women who were displaced were terrorized and angry — and also euphoric. They were ethnic Pashtuns, who lived under a strict and conservative social code. Most of them had never been outside the mud walls of their family compound more than two or three times in their lives and now here they are, hundreds or thousand of kilometres from home in this totally new situation and its scary as hell and they were fascinated. They were living in camps — and of course that was difficult and it was upsetting — but it was also fascinating: they huddled in the doors of their tents, holding the drapes closed with just space for their eyes, and they feasted on all this unfamiliar activity. They had access to medical care, some for the first time; and their daughters were going to classes run in the camps by UNICEF and Save the Children; and the women themselves were being invited to all-female classes to learn some skills that would allow them to earn a small income. Of course they were angry that the government was bombing their villages, of course they were horrified to be living in a camp with a public latrine, but it was also really, really exciting.

I discovered this by talking to them: by going into their tents and into the houses where they were displaced and meeting those women. This was not an easy story for me to do either. First of all, I had to persuade men, because I'm treated like an honorary man, so I was talking to men, and I had to persuade them that I wanted to talk these women. So, I'd say, "Can I ask your wife what she thinks, can I ask your daughters what they think?" They would respond, "Oh, they don't know anything. They got nothing to tell you. You don't want to talk them." I'd say, "I know, I know, I know but can I just talk to them for a minute?"

I did that over and over. And eventually I got in the room, or into the tents, or the one room in the house where the women are. But then I can't talk to them: they don't speak English. Often Arabic is the one language I'll have in common with people in Muslim societies, but these women have limited literacy and they don't know Arabic, and I can't find any women who speak Pashtun and also English or Arabic; I needed male translators. So I sat in the tent with the women, and my translator sat outside. "Sadiq, ask her how she felt when the Taliban took over her village?" He yells into the tent. She yells something long and very angry in Pashto back out through the wall. He yells back to me, "She says that she's really angry that they closed the school!" Once he stood on a ladder in the alley and we all spoke through the window screen; I wrote at the time that it was like being in a Catholic confessional, but a lot more crowded.

It was a very hard story for me to do but if I'd been a man I would never have done it at all. I would not have been able to talk to those women. I would not have been permitted to be in the room with them. I never would have seen the grins on their faces under their burkas. I would never have seen their faces. The story that I wrote was about how the displacement of these two million people offered a potential huge challenge to the social mores of the whole region, and that was a story that in the long run could be as or more important as any story about military strategy.

So rule number three is Be a Woman.

Now despite the miracles of modern science, obviously becoming a woman is not an option open to many of you. For those of you who aren't women and who don't feel you can remedy that problem, I would suggest that as a second-best measure, you remember, always, how easy it is to not hear women's voices, and that you need to make an effort, sometimes a heroic effort, to hear the other half of the story.

Rule #4: Manage Your Rage

I have, as a personal hero, a woman named Martha Gellhorn, with whom some of you may be familiar. Martha was one of the great war correspondents of the twentieth century. She made her name as a war reporter in the Spanish Civil War, and through the ensuing decades right up until her death in 1998 she continued to cover conflicts and disasters. She was brave and she was fierce and she was a glorious writer. She pioneered a new kind of war reporting, by focusing on the victims of war, on civilians, on women and children. It's one of the great regrets of my life that I narrowly missed an opportunity to meet her before she died; my friend Anna Maria Tremonti of the CBC did get to meet her and glows when she talks about that experience.

Martha was often asked if she was ever afraid. And while I am loath to compare myself to her, I will say that I am often asked this too, and I sometimes wonder whether a male reporter would be asked it as often.

She was often asked, and she replied, "No. I feel angry every minute about everything." Starting from her coverage of homeless people and hungry children in the United States in the Great Depression, she said the great challenge for her in writing up her reporting was "eliminating as much as possible the sound of me screaming."

As I was writing this, my partner Meril looked over my shoulder and remarked dryly that my great rage, as a journalist, is directed at the editors who tell me I can only have six hundred words for a story. Which is true, but only partly.

In 2004, I travelled to the east of the Democratic Republic of Congo, where a particularly brutal war had been going on for the best part of eight years, leaving more than two and a half million people dead, most of them from starvation and other consequences of displacement. I wanted to write about the war, which it seemed to me attracted nothing like the level of attention that those sorts of numbers merited. Part of my plan was that I wanted to investigate something I had heard about this conflict — reports that every side in this inter-state, multi-actor conflict had one thing in common, and that was rape, that they used gang rape as a key weapon in their arsenal. As I set out, people — Congolese politicians and social workers, aid workers, the few human rights researchers who had looked at the problem — told me, "No one will talk to you. Women will not talk about this. To talk to a stranger about this would be a second violation. You cannot do this story, you will not be able, because no one will talk to you." So I thought, well, great. But, remember rule one: show up.

I set off into the east on a motorbike — because there were no surviving roads — and I'm a little anxious about meeting one of a half-dozen rebel groups around a bend in the track in the jungle. After two days of travelling my Congolese guide left me at the Catholic manse in a town called Kibombo. It was the only building, or part of a building, still standing. The caretaker let me in, led me down the hall with a stub of a candle, and took me into a room that was completely bare except for a bed, leaving me with the candle. I hung up my mosquito net by my earrings, because there was no hook, and I sat under it in the dark wondering — well, "what the hell," really — that's a big part of this job.

It got very dark, and then the caretaker came back and knocked at the door and told me someone was there to see me. And I thought, "Okay, I don't know anybody in Kibombo but I'm sure they're nice here." So I followed him back up the hallway and in a little room at the front of the manse there were five Congolese women waiting for me. They have their hair braided in stiff, stiff braids the way Congolese women do, they're wearing old, faded cotton wrappers, and they have bare feet with the thick, thick calluses of people who've never had shoes. I sit down and look at them and they look not quite at me, just a little bit past me. We all sit there and then the oldest one straightened her shoulders and she said, "We heard that you want to hear what happened to us," and I said, "Yes, I'd like to hear what happened to you."

Here's what they told me.

Anya was sixteen and very small. The rebels that had raided Kibombo the year before had taken her and her mother into the forest and held her there, tied to a tree, for a month, and seven or eight of them had raped her every day. Nifa, who was fifty-five years old, told me she was raped by ten government soldiers while her husband was held at gunpoint across the room. Shami was twenty-one years old and was raped with sticks and gun barrels by members of the Mai Mai gang, a paramilitary force associated with the government, while her seven-month-old son sobbed hysterically on the floor beside her. Léonie was fifty-two years old, and sat up so straight and so tall while she told me this story — as a particular twist, the soldiers who raped her made her lie down on top of the body of her father-in-law while they did it.

They talked and they talked and they talked and Anya, little Anya, slowly, eventually, near dawn, fell asleep and she slid down onto the shoulder of the woman who was sitting next to her. Everywhere I went across the eastern Congo, in every single town this happened, there were women with stories like this. All those warnings about how no one would talk to me? I ran out of paper. There was no paper to buy, in the east of Congo, and I was reduced to writing on the back of my plane tickets, I wrote on pages I tore out of a magazine I had with me.

They talked: they talked because I was the first person to ask. There was no legal system, no police force, no judicial inquiries, no authority of any kind to go to — their sole contact with the "authorities" were the Congolese army soldiers who were as implicated in gang rapes as every other force. There was no counselling, there was no therapy, there were no support groups. And there was no medical care: I met one doctor, one apologetic, rueful doctor sitting in a clinic by himself, a clinic where the window screens and the taps and the doorknobs had all been looted and he didn't have a Band-Aid. He said women come every single day, women whose cervixes have been crushed by the force of the rape, their uteruses are prolapsed by the force of rape with sticks and gun barrels. And he doesn't have so much as a Band-Aid. He doesn't have Tylenol, he has nothing. There is one doctor, this incredible man named Denis Mukwege — the one doctor in all of Congo who is trained to repair these kinds of injuries. The women would have needed to walk for about three months to get to his hospital in Bukavu. Eventually, I got there, on my motorbike — and I met them, the women who walked through the jungle for months in the hope that someone might be able to stop the steady leaking of blood and feces and urine from their bodies.

Once I got home to Johannesburg, I had all those bits of paper in front of me, and it was difficult to hear myself think over the sound of screaming in my head. I was acutely conscious in trying to write that story that I could do absolutely nothing for these women — they needed food and physical safety and medical care and a hundred other things. And I had a notebook. I could offer them journalism. I could do nothing for them.

Martha Gellhorn said, about interviewing survivors of the Nazi Holocaust, "the best I could do was remember for them." The best I could hope was that the articles I wrote might bring some small bit of attention to the war in Congo and to the way the bodies of women were being used as its battlefield.

That did not — does not — feel like very much.

Rule #5: Be Prepared to Live with the Consequences of Your Journalism
In 1999, when I had been a reporter at the *Globe* for just over a year, I

travelled to South Sudan to report on the war between the government of Sudan and the Sudan People's Liberation Army, the SPLA, which was fighting for the independence of South Sudan, and had been for nearly two decades, at the cost of more than a million lives. In particular, I was interested in the area where oil was newly being drilled — in a project headed by the Calgary-based company Talisman Energy. There were allegations that Sudanese people were being driven from their homes and farms in the area where oil was discovered, in often-brutal attacks by plainclothes militias — with the knowledge, the complicity, possibly even the assistance of the oil company — and that hundreds or maybe tens of thousands of people were now refugees from the area where this Canadian oil company had been given a concession by the government.

These were very serious allegations about a Canadian company, but they had not really been investigated: the dictatorship in Khartoum made it almost impossible for foreign journalists to get into the country, let alone into the south. The oil area was remote and really physically inaccessible. The oil company had flown a hand-picked group of journalists there on their helicopter. They had seen some nice schools that were built by the company, some wells that were dug for the local population. They didn't see any displaced people. The only other way to get to that area, to see what was happening, was to go, by oneself, in through the area that was controlled by the rebels. So that's what I decided to do with a photographer friend of mine named John Morstad. We flew up, as close as you could get, with an aid agency that occasionally took supplies in, and they left us on a dirt airstrip. The only thing that stood between us and the oil fields was a civil war and the Nile headwaters, which, I learned as we landed, originate there and flood the entire region every year, so that was good news.

We were met by guides from the civilian wing of the Sudanese liberation movement, and we walked, for a very long time, through swamp where the water was often over my head. Fortunately, this is the territory of the Dinka, the tallest people on earth, so we were able to enlist some twelve-year-old girls to carry our satellite phone and other gear on their heads when the water was deep — they were about eight feet tall. They walked through the swamps and I swam, thanking my parents mentally for all the swimming lessons when I was a child. We eventually reached the outer edges of the oil fields, although not until my toenails had begun to rot and fall off. There we met large numbers of obviously displaced people living in a dire situation, unassisted by aid groups, and they told me stories about being driven out of their homes. There was one woman who told me a searing story, which still haunts me, about running in the night when her home was set on fire by men on horseback with torches; she ran, carrying her three-year-old and her toddler. She ran and ran through the night but eventually she was too tired to carry them both and she had to decide which child to put down and leave and which child she would continue to carry while she ran.

Many people told us about white men driving the pickup trucks of the raiders but we didn't see that and we couldn't prove it. Obviously we were conscious at all times that the rebel movement had a version of this story that they wanted us to hear, to believe. It was certainly possible to establish there was a serious humanitarian situation here at the edge of the oil field and that Talisman needed to stop denying the existence of this humanitarian situation and start investigating it or explaining it.

Footnote three: after about a week in the region it was time for John and me to head back south, to catch another aid flight out. As we were leaving the village where we'd been camped, a senior fighter came to see us off. He was hobbling, leaning on a stick with stained yellow bandages wrapped around his foot. I asked what was wrong, and he said he'd been bitten by a snake. I said, "Not anywhere around here, I hope?" And he said, "Oh yes, just here actually," and gestured into the swamp that we were about to wade into. And I think, "Fantastic!" My toenails have already fallen off. I hadn't thought about snakes. But he sees me looking very worried and he says, "No, no, don't worry, the wound isn't from the snake bite." And I was very relieved, and said, "Oh good." And he said, "Oh no. The wound is from where I set my foot on fire so that the snake venom wouldn't kill me." (Rule number six: always travel with waterproof matches.)

So I looked at John and said, "Okay, when a snake gets me, you set my foot on fire because I'm not going to be able to set my own foot on fire. I'll set your foot on fire, you set my foot on fire." We had a little deal.

To return to rule number five, John and I made it back to Toronto unbitten, and we put together an article that the *Globe* ran over two full pages. It was certainly not the only spur for, but it was an important contribution to, a nascent shareholder action in Canada against Talisman; it was one of the more successful such movements in recent Canadian economic history. Talisman was forced by public pressure to divest. They said it had to do with the cost of running the concession and a lot of other things, but the opinion of analysts I've talked to about this is that the shareholder action, the public pressure about what they were doing in Sudan, forced them to divest and they had to get out of South Sudan.

That's a good exercise in journalism, right? It's going somewhere, doing everything you can to hear multiple sides of the story as objectively as possible, and contributing to an improvement in the situation of some very marginalized people who had no ability to speak for themselves, right? Wrong. Because Talisman sold their stake in those oil fields to the petroleum companies of India and China. And there went any digging of wells and building of schools and there went any possibility of holding anybody accountable for the human rights of the civilians who lived on the oil fields. A decade later, I still feel sick whenever I think about that story.

In Conclusion
The rules that I've laid out for you — five or maybe six if we count the matches — are obviously a little bit facetious. It is difficult, though not impossible, to show up, and get in deep, unless someone is paying your bills. I'm very, very lucky that the *Globe* still pays my bills, that it's a paper that still cares about foreign coverage. They are opening bureaus when virtually every other media organization in the developed world is closing bureaus and reducing its commitment to foreign coverage. *Globe* readers, God love them, much like CBC listeners, still want foreign coverage. It's still something that *Globe* readers ask for and that makes it possible for

me to do my job and I'm profoundly grateful for that. Nevertheless, the foreign correspondent is a badly endangered species. In fact, for a small fee I'm willing to pose for photos with you in the lobby if you want one to show your grandchildren. "Look Susie, a correspondent for a newspaper!" Oh, you laugh.

Look, I love Twitter — it's been my chief source of breaking news for a couple of years now. I love my Flip, an idiot-proof pocket-size video camera, and YouTube, and all the things these new technologies make possible. I love the citizen journalist. We most often talk about them in the context of events such as the G20 protests in Toronto, when hundreds of people could photograph police behaviour on their cellphones and post the pictures on their blogs. That stuff is important.

But for me the greater value of innovations like this lies in people like a guy named Chelapila Santakar, who I met last year when I travelled to the heart of India's Maoist insurgency. (Yes, Maoists. Who knew there are still Maoists?) It took days and days of travel through jungles and over land-mined roads to get there, and I was only the second journalist working for a mainstream media outlet to go, in more than a year, despite the fact that hundreds of thousands of people now live under the rule of the Naxalites, to this Maoist rebel movement. But Santakar lives in the middle of it, and with a very basic point-and-shoot camera, and a dial-up Internet connection, he provides a daily stream of reporting from a conflict that India's government would prefer that you not know about and not pay attention to. That's citizen journalism of an absolutely amazing kind, and it's also coming out of northern Uganda and Tibet and a hundred other places, and we didn't hear those voices or hear that news unfold five years ago.

I find this stuff exhilarating. The stuff Santakar does in his little office just gave me goosebumps. I thought: this is so important. But I guess the point that I'd like to make tonight is that there is also value in the oldest of old media, in going there and going deep and really listening — and then, with the benefit of perspective, reporting it in a format of more than one hundred and forty characters and even more than six hundred words. There is value in reflection and there is value in analysis. We all want to know these days where our carrots come from and who grew them. You should also want to know where your news came from and who's telling it to you. That kind of journalism produces stories that you need as much or more than you need from the news stream that you get from Facebook.

Let's do a quick survey. Could you put your hand up, please, and leave it up if you have an iPhone? A Blackberry? A plain-old cellphone from the Superstore? A laptop computer? A desktop? A Wii? A Sony PlayStation? Okay, so that leaves two of you. You can put your hands down now. For all the rest of you, except those two people, let me tell you the other thing that I didn't mention about those women in the Congo that I told you about. The rebels and the government soldiers who raped Anya and Shami and Leoni, they were fighting over their village and trying to terrorize and suppress that civilian population because Kibombo sits in the middle of Congo's mineral fields. The area where they live is full of coltan. Coltan is the mineral that makes our electronics work. It's in my Blackberry and it's in your Mac and it's in your PlayStation. And 80 percent of the coltan in our consumer electronics comes from the DRC. You are, we are, the reason that there is a war in eastern Congo. We are the reason that there is an unending epidemic of rape there.

For those of you who are journalism students, you can do this, regardless of what this job looks like in five years or ten years. I don't know what it's going to look like, but you can tell these stories and the world is going to need to hear them more than ever. These are stories we need to hear and they are stories you can go and tell.

Q: My name is Cedric Noel. I've lived in various countries around the world. My parents both work for NGOs. And my question to you is, you've faced a lot of challenges and a lot of advantages to being a woman reporter, but what challenges and what advantages did you have being a foreign reporter in a foreign country?

A: That's a great question, Cedric. You know it's a complete mixed bag. You get access in some ways because you're foreign and you're always up against a culture you don't really know, often a language you don't speak.

There are a thousand things going on in the conversation that a local reporter would catch, that I don't catch, right? It's at least a thousand and I'm always very conscious of that. I could spend the rest of my life in eastern Congo and I still wouldn't really know what's going on, right? So that's a disadvantage. I get access that I wouldn't necessarily get if I worked for local media and I have the ability to report honestly about things that often local journalists just don't have. That story in Zimbabwe was a key example. I know a lot of amazing, amazing Zimbabwean journalists who could kick my ass in sheer reporting ability but who if they tried to do the stories I did would have gone to jail and not got out. So that's a huge advantage.

Q: Hi I'm Brianna and I'm a third-year journalism student. My interests lay in war correspondence and after listening to you the one major question I had is: How do you come home at the end of the day and deal with everything? I know that myself and some other students started to tear up when you talked about the women in the Congo. How do you come home and deal with that?

A. Gin.
  You know I'd rather know than not know. If it's happening I'd rather go there than not go there. My personal thing is that I can't live with not knowing and not doing anything about it and not hearing about it. And I would rather spend horrific hours listening to Congolese women tell me about what was done to them than not hear their stories, and I think there is, in a very perverse way, there is greater comfort in actually hearing about it than not. But maybe I am heading for a nervous breakdown of epic proportions. No, look, the very simple fact is I have got nothing to complain about, right? It didn't happen to me. I get to go home. I get to go home to my plumbing. I am reminded every single second in my job how incredibly, incredibly, incredibly lucky I am and how privileged I am and I have got absolutely no right to feel shitty. None.

Q. You were talking about journalism and I think that journalism is the act of storytelling but in a sense, when you're going to these places, learning about all the different facts, getting all the things on paper, aren't you story-conveying rather than storytelling? Also: how many pieces of paper did you bring to the Congo?

A. I took three standard reporter notebooks, which usually I take three for every two-week, three-week trip. Two should be enough and I have the extra one in case I lose one and I burned through those, in like, a night. So it's a very good question: I was responsible, I did bring paper, I just brought more than enough for the usual trip. It just wasn't enough. You are totally right about the conveying. The best stories that I've ever done, including that one, I just wrote it down. I did nothing else. The story that I wrote, now seven years ago, was about a woman in Rwanda named Athanasie Mukarwego. She was raped for months by the Interahamwe during the genocide in Rwanda and all I did with that story was, I essentially transcribed. Athanasie told me that story, and I put it in the paper word-for-word — in her words — and all I did was write it down. In the best stuff I've done, all I did was write it down.

September 29, 2010

NEIL REYNOLDS

The Last Commandment: Thou Shall Not Beguile

Neil Reynolds dropped out of high school to work for a newspaper, and over a long career became one of the great editors of newspapers in Canada. He was editor of the Kingston Whig-Standard, *the New* Brunswick Telegraph-Journal *and* Saint John Times Globe, *the* Ottawa Citizen, *and the* Vancouver Sun. *He was an inspiring and courageous leader in a newsroom. I know this to be true because I worked in some of his newsrooms, where he told us that we were producing the literature of the people, and that most of all, literature should be memorable. At the end of his career, he shared his time between Ottawa and New Brunswick, as editor-at-large for Brunswick News Inc. and writing a column for the* Globe and Mail. *We cornered him for this talk during an east coast leg of his travels. Reynolds died on May 19, 2013.*

I do want to say, up front, that — speaking of Anonymous — I do not know who wrote the collected works of William Shakespeare. I prefer to think that Shakespeare wrote them — for the very reason that some scholars think he didn't. How could a commoner write such majestic verse? I think that Matthew Arnold, the melancholy English poet, captured this paradox best in a sonnet dedicated to the Bard: "And thou, self-schooled, self-scanned, self-honoured, self-secure, didst tread on earth unguessed at: Better so!"

Mark Twain is a lesser, though exalted, example of the prodigious accomplishments of the self-taught commoner. Born Samuel Clemens, the boy quit school at age twelve to take a full-time job as a printer's apprentice, as a typesetter, in Hannibal, Missouri. (For quick comparison, Max Aitken, yet another self-taught commoner, was thirteen when — a generation or so later — he published *The Reader*, his first newspaper.) Twain educated himself by reading, at night, in the Hannibal public library. And why not? As he later put it, the library had more books than the school. It was enough to equip him for his brief, ambivalent career in journalism. If you don't read newspapers, he once said, you will be uninformed. If you do read them, you will be misinformed. More to the point, he acutely observed, "There is no suffering comparable with that which a private person feels when he is, for the first time, pilloried in print."

There is truth in these judgments, which acknowledge the fact that newspapers are the only business in the world to publish a complete record of all their mistakes. Yet now, with the end of the *News of the World*, the closing of Rupert Murdoch's scandalous Sunday tabloid, the scales that weigh journalism's mischief and malfeasance have tilted from libel, the act of reporting falsehood, to hacking, the act of reporting truth. Supreme Court Chief Justice Beverley McLachlin noted the distinction herself in a 2009 ruling. Libel actions deal primarily with published statements that are false, she observed. Privacy actions deal primarily with published statements that are true.

Legislatures and courts have not yet determined which is the greater wrong — the fiction or the fact, the defamatory falsehood or the clandestine truth. Either can be regarded as a crime and punished by the state. Either can be regarded as a mere wrong, and avenged in civil court. As always, it depends. WikiLeaks is one thing, *Hello!* magazine's acquisition of Michael Douglas and Catherine Zeta-Jones's wedding pictures is another thing altogether.

Journalistic libels are usually legally serious only when committed maliciously, a motive mostly absent in journalistic hacking. Yet civil courts are the best way to deal with both kinds of wrongdoing. Civil courts are adept at calculating precise damages — an essential skill in proceedings based on assertions of "irreparable harm." It is this skill that enables judges to award complainants one dollar in damages for marginally malicious libels. Some people, after all, have no reputations left to lose. And some people have no private lives left to live.

People do exaggerate the gravity of the privacy violations done to them. Take the Douglas-Zeta-Jones wedding in New York in 2000. Mr. Douglas and Ms. Zeta-Jones had sold to Britain's *OK!* magazine (for $1.6 million) the world rights to the wedding photographs. Notwithstanding stringent privacy precautions, *Hello!* obtained and published pictures of the ceremony.

In the ensuing civil action, which took eight years and cost $8 million, Mr. Douglas and Ms. Zeta-Jones predictably asserted, with some exaggeration, that *Hello!*'s transgressions had caused them "irreparable harm." In the end, the court ordered the magazine to pay them $25,000. More significantly, it fined the magazine $170 for its violation of England's Data Protection Act. At $170 per transgression, this penalty could be taken as encouragement to hack.

Please don't misinterpret: the rogue reporters in England who hacked the cellphones of children, war veterans, prime ministers, and princes committed acts of appalling moral wrong. But the injury that they caused was, for the most part, limited. It does not justify criminal prosecution by the state. Better to leave these wrongs for the civil courts — where punishment can be expected, with great precision, to fit the offence.

For journalistic purposes, hacking began long ago, with the shoving of brown envelopes under reporters' doors. But in a society in which everyone is a journalist of one kind or another, technology has radically democratized the practice. An email arrived in my inbox the other day with this offer in the subject line: "read the secret files of your wife." The message promoted a service that promised to deliver "invisible, anonymous and fully undetectable electronic surveillance" of any computer — hence, any person — in the world. We are, alas, not far from the emergence of computer hacking as a service industry. Indeed, some journalists already regard hacking as an integral part of their skill sets. In *Hack Journalism*, Argentine author Pablo Mancini says, "there can be no journalism without hackers."

Newspapers certainly aren't what they used to be and it's still not certain what they will be. But the best of them remain authoritative, informative, and, here and there, profitable. Yes, many newspapers are still in decline. Newspapers thrived when news was a scarce commodity. News is now everywhere abundant, and essentially free for the taking. But make no mistake. The print newspaper remains a close friend for hundreds of millions of people around the world, ironically making it a social medium in its own unique way.

According to an Ipsos-Reid poll this year, however, only thirty percent of Canadians express any significant level of trust in journalists themselves. Asked to rate different professions on a trust scale of one to seven (with seven indicating the highest trust), only three out of ten respondents marked journalists as five, six, or seven. This put them slightly ahead of TV personalities, union leaders, environmental activists, CEOs — and national politicians. But national politicians increased their positive rating by sixteen percentage points in seven years, journalists by only one percentage point.

Aside from the friendship that forms from physical contact, experienced daily and extended across lifetimes, print newspapers are definitely not a social medium. Properly experienced, they are a medium of separation: of transient reflection, of surreptitious contemplation and, occasionally, of devout meditation. This may not appear to be much but it is, in fact, important. In its solitary aloneness, the print newspaper makes a unique contribution to civilized life, to community life, in our democracy — or in any democracy. This contribution is now threatened — not so much by neat technologies, as we tend to think, as by a lack of trustworthiness. It is not clear whether it is primarily our remaining readers who don't trust us, or whether it is primarily the readers we have already lost. Either way, we need to take trust as seriously as we take technology. I propose a first, humble reform: that newspapers stop publishing, completely, once and for all, comment or content provided by anonymous sources.

This is a controversial proposition. The anonymous source has been thoroughly romanticized. As we all know, or think we know, Deep Throat brought down Richard Nixon — and Richard Nixon deserved to be brought down. Now, it is true that Nixon fell for reasons that transcended Watergate. As legendary *Washington Post* executive editor Ben Bradlee once put it, Nixon had no style — "none whatsoever." But whatever the extraneous aspects to Nixon's fall, there remains a hypothetical chance that another president (or prime minister) may need to be taken down one day. If so, most journalists insist, they will want to have all of their arrows in their quivers: close at hand.

I have argued for many years that newspapers are the scriptures of our secular times. In this metaphor, it will take a miracle to restore the people's trust. One of our problems is that we distanced ourselves too far from objective journalism: telling, as fairly and honestly as humanly possible, the other side of the story. Indeed, we distanced ourselves deliberately. Since no person can be perfectly objective, we said, objective reporting is *Mission: Impossible*. In the sense that no journalist is omniscient, I agree. In the sense that we shouldn't try hard for objectivity anyway, I disagree. After all, we seek to print the truth — and we do sign our names to our work.

Thus my homily begins. Let the blogosphere do what it must in its own anarchic way. Let print journalism clean up its act — and go, if we must go, honourably. My first text is taken from *Reminiscences*, the memoirs of John Stephen Willison, editor of the *Toronto Globe* for the final two decades of the nineteenth century. For our purposes, this reading is from Genesis.

In the beginning, John Stephen Willison was born in 1856 on an isolated frontier farm in Upper Canada. "The house in which I was born stood in a clearing and all around was woods in which no axe had ever swung," he recalled. "As a child, I often wandered among thick underbrush, and picked wild flowers along streams that ceased to murmur long ago. We knew the bush could be loud and angry, for we had heard the great trees wail in the storms. But for the most part, we looked into deep and friendly silences. We saw the earth unspoiled by human artifice, as when 'God saw everything that He had made and, behold, it was good.'" This was Eden, or Eden enough.

The Fall always begins innocently. For Willison, it was the poems and the letters to the editor that he submitted anonymously, as a lad with a literary bent, to the small-town newspapers that covered the countryside of nineteenth-century Canada. Willison described his first published work as a "mood poem of portentous solemnity." Fortunately, he remarked retrospectively, the *Whitby Chronicle* did not survive and its archives were not preserved. His second published work was a letter to the editor of the *Guelph Mercury* on prohibition. He was in favour. "I expressed a weighty opinion," he recalled. "I forget whether I wrote my name as 'Total Abstinence,' 'Pioneer,' 'Ratepayer' or 'Pro Bono Publico.' Any one of these signatures, though, would have carried more authority than my own."

Here was Willison's first confession. As far as I can determine, only two reasons exist for pseudonyms in journalism. The first is Willison's: pretence. The second is fear. The first, I think, cannot be justified; the second only for people who do not possess freedom of speech — the Arab Spring insurgents in the Middle East in the twenty-first century, the samizdat dissidents in the Soviet Union in the twentieth, perhaps even the Brontë sisters in England in the nineteenth — who first published their disturbing reports of family life in England as novels and, as if that were not protection enough, as the work of three brothers, Currer Bell (for Charlotte), Ellis Bell (for Emily), and Acton Bell (for Anne).

In some cases, the two justifications co-exist: for example, the clandestine eighteenth-century writers of the Federalist Papers in the United States — Alexander Hamilton, James Madison, and John Jay. They published their critique of the draft American constitution as "Publius," simultaneously evoking "the people" and the Roman consul who overthrew the monarchy and established a republic. These distinguished American writers felt obliged to publish anonymously because, as they said — and this is a common excuse for anonymity — they feared "a detrimental effect on employment."

Suffice it to note that one writer's resort to anonymity induces further anonymity. Thus the critics of the Federalist Papers, themselves distinguished, included such people as "Brutus" and "Cato." And for what point? Benjamin

Franklin, who didn't use pseudonyms, described his anonymous brethren as "a bunch of misguided souls who don't understand that the whole point of writing is self-promotion."

But back to Willison. Self-taught and "full of ambition," the young writer proceeded from anonymous letters to the editorship — 1880 through 1902 — of the (Toronto) *Globe*, a remarkable achievement, even for an enthusiastic Liberal partisan in an age of advanced political chicanery. In 1913, King George V knighted him, toward the end of his career, for his contribution to Canadian journalism. (For quick comparison, King George knighted Max Aitken in 1911 and made him a lord of the realm, as Baron Beaverbrook, in 1917.) Willison remains the only working-class stiff — he called himself a mere paragrapher — ever so ennobled.

In his stint in the parliamentary press gallery in Ottawa, before becoming editor of the *Globe*, Willison's first assignment was to befriend Wilfrid Laurier — one might say, to beguile him. Laurier was a rising Liberal star; destined, four years later, to become the leader of the Liberal Party; destined, four years later still, to become prime minister. Willison succeeded in his assignment, though it took him a full year to do it. The two men became close friends and formidable allies and the *Globe* gained an important anonymous source.

This was how they practised journalism in the old days. The *London Advertiser* assigned Willison, as a novice reporter, to "nose" political meetings — to hide his identify as a reporter and to gather political intelligence "by guile." In his memoirs, Willison references journalistic guile almost as often as he references journalistic wile. The two words, of course, mean the same thing and trace etymologically to witchcraft and sorcery.

On the one hand, Willison was a principled man, utterly honourable. On the other hand, as journalist, he could privately pledge to Laurier that he was prepared to render "any service" to help the Liberal leader win Ontario in the next election. And he did render service. In the election of 1891, for example, he blocked publication of material, supplied by the former Liberal leader, Edward Blake, that could have proven highly damaging to Laurier, who didn't win the election but who came close. (And in the next election, of course, he did win.)

How much information did the journalists of the day keep secret to protect anonymous sources in high places? By Willison's account, they hid a lot — and took much of it to their graves. "There is truth in the old statement that history is a lie," he said. "There is much that the contemporary writer cannot divulge. I think of the events within my own knowledge of which I can say little or nothing. Of the real pith of these events, neither this generation nor any other generation can have full or exact knowledge."

Yet paradoxically, for Willison, the journalist's task remained sacred. "What is the true mission of the journalist, whether one confesses it or not, but to find the Balm of Gilead for the distresses of his time?...If one does not possess this evangelical spirit, and strive to make the world cleaner and better, what profit hath he [Ecclesiastes 2:22] 'of all his labour wherein he laboureth under the sun?'" The true journalist, Willison insists, is most happy when reporting on the wickedness of things — though the definition of wicked, he notes, can change remarkably over time. "A generation ago, it required courage for a newspaper to attack a group of capitalists," he said. "Now it requires even greater courage to defend [them]."

Herein lies a great truth: as daily journals of moral conduct, each successive edition is another chapter of a holy book. On a global scale, we are still supplementing Lamentations at a rapid rate. Whether locally, regionally, or nationally, though, all newspapers supplement the scriptures in the same way: by reporting what's gone wrong, by reporting what's gone right, and by leaving readers to ponder the morality of it — that is, whose job it is to fix what's broken and whose job it is to pay for the fix.

This is serious work. And this is why I lament the bizarre media obsession these days with trivially anonymous quotations from the Web. Many news organizations routinely report anonymous tweets as an integral part of their news reports. (CNN, I understand; CBC, I don't understand.) Remarkably, the journalists who read these missives on-air appear minimally embarrassed and maximally enthusiastic. Further, many news organizations aid and abet rampant anonymity on their websites. Who are these people who require anonymity to express commonplace, everyday opinions? Why the pretence? Why the fear? It was for this that our ancestors fought and died for freedom of speech? It is for this that thirty-six journalists around the world have died so far this year in the line of duty?

Examined from a different perspective, you could pose a different question. Who would go to church to hear a sermon read by a masked preacher? The irony here is that the press replaced the preacher long ago — and now, because it doesn't truly understand its moral purpose, risks losing its own congregation. One writer who recognized this transition early on was a nineteenth-century English reformer named James Leatham. Writing in 1892, Leatham argued that the press had already supplanted the pulpit for every function except ceremonial rites. The press, in other words, had already taken over all responsibility for moral instruction and had left for the preacher only the baptisms, weddings, and funerals.

"The press is not perfect," Leatham conceded, "but, with all its faults, it represents the people. Forced by the conditions of its existence to please those for whom it caters, it reflects every mood of the public. It is all things to all men. It finds out everything; it tells everything it finds out."

The influence of the pulpit waned, Leatham said, because the preacher spoke on old and outworn themes — "because the public's interest in Abraham, Isaac, and Jacob paled before the public's interest in Tom, Dick, and Harry." And, we might add, in Angelina, Brad, and Jennifer — and in all the celebrities whose lives now provide incomparable parables of compelling moral instruction.

"The press has accomplished much in a short space of time," Leatham wrote. "The pulpit has accomplished less in a long career. What the press has done, it has done despite the hostility of princes and the repression of Parliaments. What the pulpit has failed to do, it has failed to do notwithstanding the favour of princes or the subsidies of Parliaments. In influence for civilization and enlightenment, the press, with all its faults, leaves the pulpit helplessly, ignominiously in the shade."

Two themes emerge. On the one hand, the journalist is — Willison's word — evangelist: the teller of the gospel truth. On the other hand, the journalist is — Leatham's word — preacher: the person who publicly proclaims. If the journalists had indeed already replaced the preachers at the turn of the twentieth century, what do we really mean when we speak of the separation of church and state? Do we not necessarily imply a comparable separation of press and state? There are two distinctly disruptive issues here. The first is the journalist who knows the gospel truth and declines to tell it. The second is the journalist who doesn't know the gospel truth but who passes along anonymous versions of it.

For this latter journalist, different levels of anonymity have been developed, the most extreme of which is American journalism's "deep background," which requires the journalist to not identify the source in any way, however slightly. When a journalist goes onto "deep background," he or she quotes the anonymous source verbatim — as a matter of fact. In *Game Change*, a 2010 account of the U.S. presidential election of 2008, political journalists John Heilemann and Mark Halperin set a record of some kind by quoting more than two hundred sources anonymously — all of them on "deep background."

Most newspapers have adopted rules for "deep background" reporting but the exceptions are many — and the abuses alarming. One notorious example was *Newsweek* magazine's anonymous report, May 15, 2005, that U.S. guards at Guantanamo had flushed a Koran down a toilet "in an attempt to rattle suspects" for interrogation purposes. In reporting this incident, the magazine said that "unnamed sources" — plural — had verified the information. In fact, the incident never happened. Yet seventeen people died in the ensuing demonstrations throughout the Muslim world. When *Newsweek* apologized two weeks later, it was expressing its regret, as former U.S. Defense Secretary Donald Rumsfeld put it, "to people who were already dead."

The point, of course, is this: when anonymous sources err, newspapers err. When anonymous sources lie, newspapers lie. In either event, newspapers that use anonymous sources risk further loss of the public's trust. It happens, as the *Washington Post*'s Ben Bradlee has conceded, "all the time." Access to powerful people, Bradlee says, gives privileged reporters an opportunity to delve deeper in the search for truth. But it also gives these reporters an opportunity to manipulate the truth — "a little, a lot or beyond all recognition."

Bradlee became executive editor of the *Post* in 1968, the year Nixon first won election as president. When he retired in 1991, he spoke extensively, in a public lecture, on anonymous-source manipulation of journalists. In this lecture, Bradlee traced the rise of modern anonymous-source journalism to Theodore White, the journalist who wrote *The Making of the President: 1960*, an immensely successful book that set the standard for quick-hit journalistic biographies. Kennedy gave White unprecedented access to himself, his wife, and his advisers. White explicitly portrayed Kennedy as an Arthurian hero, the Kennedy White House as Camelot — a mythology, which White later repented, that survives to this day.

White's successes — political advantage for Kennedy, journalistic advantage for himself — persuaded other politicians to swap intimate access for favourable coverage. "The great manipulation madness," Bradlee said, "was underway." Here's a verse or two from the gospel according to Ben Bradlee:

"My thesis is not that access [to the high and mighty] breeds manipulation," he said, "although it damn well can. My thesis is that the manipulators have gone way beyond the granting of access or the withholding of access in their campaign to influence, and thereby distort, reality. And we in the press have shown remarkably little righteous indignation about it. I'm not talking about exaggerating, misrepresenting, misspeaking. I'm talking about the real McCoy: lying."

Bradlee proceeded to indict every president since Eisenhower of strategic lying: the elder Bush, Reagan, Carter, Ford, Nixon, Johnson, Kennedy. Were he speaking today, he would undoubtedly include Obama, the younger Bush, and Clinton. Some of these lies are now infamous. Campaigning on his honesty, Jimmy Carter assured the American people: "I'll never lie to you." According to Bradlee, it was his first lie.

But are we really shocked that political leaders lie? I don't think so. We are too cynical — or, rather, we are properly cynical. But what do these lies mean if politicians live and lie by a different moral code than the rest of us? This is Jane Jacobs's argument in *Systems of Survival: A Dialogue on the Moral Foundations of Commerce and Politics*. In this humble little 1994 manifesto, Jacobs asserts that politicians are hard-wired to lie. For the most part, Jacobs says, politicians believe — they honestly believe — that lying for a political purpose, "for the sake of the task," is morally justified. And for politicians, the highest task is the pursuit and preservation of power.

In *Systems of Survival*, using newspaper stories as parables, Jacobs identifies two distinct moral syndromes that, she says, have governed humanity through the ages. The first of these is the guardian syndrome: the profession, or the class, of politics and government. The second is the commercial syndrome: the profession, or the class, of trade and commerce. What is moral in one is not necessarily moral in the other. What is immoral in one is not necessarily immoral in the other.

Jacobs identified traits that she associated with each of these moral syndromes. Call them, as she did, guardian and trader — or, call them, more simply, raider and trader.

Here are Jacobs's trader-class indicators: you shun force. You seek voluntary agreements and you respect them. You are honest. You collaborate easily with strangers. You are competitive. You value initiative and enterprise. You are open to novelty and inventiveness. You value efficiency. You are industrious. You are thrifty. You are optimistic.

Here are Jacobs's guardian-class indicators: you shun commerce. You exert prowess. You are disciplined. You are obedient. You value tradition. You respect hierarchy. You are loyal. You make rich use of leisure. You are fatalistic. You treasure personal honour. And, finally, you deceive for the sake of the task.

Jacobs says that we do need to recognize a more formal separation of these syndromes: separation of church and state, certainly; but separation of commerce and state as well — perhaps we can call it separation of store and state. But, again, what are we to make of journalists? Are we guardians? Are we guardians of the guardians? Is this why we are morally comfortable with anonymous-source deceit — and deception for the sake of the task?

Or are we traders? Several traits suggest it. We operate in the market-place — and depend on it for our very survival. We buy and sell. We are comfortable with strangers. We do not discriminate. We love to compete. And we do not, on our editorial page, justify deception for the sake of the task.

Jacobs insisted that guardian and trader tasks require different skills and different values. The trader may lie — but violates the trader code when he or she does. The guardian may run companies and manage corporations — but violates the guardian code when he or she does. But the guardian ethic permits dishonesty and, indeed, a certain ruthlessness. "I used to think of government — meaning good government — as the major force at work in the civilizing process," Jacobs said. "Now I'm inclined to think of government as being essentially barbaric — barbaric in its origins and forever susceptible to barbaric actions and aims. But don't get me wrong. We need it."

It is instructive to look, through Jacobs's lens, at the most successful of our prime ministers — most recently, Trudeau, Mulroney, Chrétien, and Harper — all of whom possessed (or possess) pronounced guardian traits. Journalists indeed described these men as dictators of a democratic sort. Lawrence Martin, in *Iron Man: The Defiant Reign of Jean Chrétien*, styled Chrétien as king. Jeffrey Simpson, in *The Friendly Dictatorship*, suggested that Chrétien proved Canada's preference for authoritarian governments.

In fact, of course, the first manifestation of guardian morality in this country was Sir John A. Macdonald himself — he who anonymously wrote news stories and editorials (and even supplied headlines, too) for the *Leader*, the Conservative paper in Toronto. Indeed, Sir John's corrupt practices — bribery, bid-rigging, vote-buying — fit Jacobs's criteria perfectly. All were explicitly for the sake of the task; none was for personal enrichment. Sir John would not have quibbled in any way with Laurier's rebuke of John Stephen Willison, his friend at the *Globe*, when Laurier and Willison ultimately parted ways. Laurier had asked Willison to stop campaigning for certain reforms. Willison felt that he had already silenced himself too much. Laurier replied with the irrefutable observation that reform was the job of opposition parties — that the job of government was survival.

It isn't that only political leaders deceive. Far from it. The Reuters-Thomson *Handbook for Journalists* says, quite correctly, that "every source who talks with a Reuters reporter has a motive [so] be wary of even trusted sources." Reuters policy nevertheless permits the use of anonymous sources — except in a single instructive instance. The Reuters handbook says: "No story about Reuters may contain a quote from an anonymous source." In this application of principle, the Reuters rule takes precedence over the Golden Rule.

The Bible, of course, is itself an anthology of anonymous writers. Biblical authorities say that the only credibly bylined work in the Good Book are the letters written by the apostle Paul — unless you think, as legend attests, that Moses wrote Genesis, Exodus, Leviticus, Numbers, and Deuteronomy himself. This confusion has not significantly hurt the Bible but then it isn't in quite the same position as newspapers. For one thing, our readers do not regard us as divinely inspired.

So why are we doing what we're doing? Publishing anonymous letters? Anonymous blogs? Anonymous politicians? The *News of the World* was the big newspaper scandal of the year, of course: a virulent contagion of journalistic knavery. But responsible Canadian journalists have as much to learn from the misuse of unnamed sources as irresponsible British journalists. The Supreme Court of Canada ruled last year that journalists have no constitutional right to shield the identity of anonymous sources — thus making it morally and legally dubious, if not altogether wrong, to promise anonymity to anyone, ever. Each case, the Court said, must be judged on its own merits — a judgment not known in advance.

Why can't the courts give journalists the right to shield the identity of anonymous sources? Because such a right would have to be extended to every writer — and who isn't a writer, these days? — in the country. Such an expansive right would entrench a licence to libel. The Supreme Court limitation is correct. In any event, journalists should never aspire to legal privileges not shared by everyone. If we are the Fourth Estate, we must be so as commoners.

A final argument. Anonymity is a kind of cowardice, highly contagious. We are witness to a pandemic of it. Journalists should try diligently to persuade reluctant sources to speak on the record; and print journalists should try hardest of all — because it's probably already game over in the other news media. It is left to print journalism to encourage courage and, indeed, to compel courage. From courage, perhaps, will come credibility.

Allan Fotheringham, the famously irreverent Canadian journalist, published his own memoirs, *A Boy from Nowhere*, last month. In his long career, he covered eleven prime ministers. Interviewed on TV the other day, Dr. Foth portrayed the political journalist in this country as manipulated — and, at the same time, as manipulator. Common practice is for journalists to inflate politicians, he said, and then, when they are fully inflated, to stick them with pins. Asked what advice he would give young journalists, he advised, stay away from the liars. Don't get "sucked in" by prime ministers and cabinet ministers. And, "Be more truthful." In other words, don't beguile — and don't be guiled. That's good advice. Journalists need to tell people everything they know, but only what they know: the gospel truth.

November 17, 2011

NAHLAH AYED

Yes, I Will Wait: In Praise of Long Journeys,
Long Interviews, and Longer Stays

In the fall of 2012, Nahlah Ayed was based in London and covering the world for the CBC. Her stories were filed from Riyadh and Tehran, Beirut and Baghdad, India, Pakistan, Kenya, and Haiti. For a decade, she lived in and covered the Middle East for the CBC. Her book, A Thousand Farewells: A Reporter's Journey from Refugee Camp to the Arab Spring, *tells the story of her journey from Winnipeg to a refugee camp in Jordan, which formed the foundation of her life as a foreign correspondent. Days after she visited the campus she was back in Egypt, reporting from Tahrir Square.*

It's quite unnerving to be standing here tonight where some of Canada's luminaries and icons in journalism have stood. It's appropriate, because as you are marking the tenth anniversary of this lecture series, I'm marking my tenth year since I left for the Middle East back in 2002, around Christmas time, going from Ottawa to Amman on to Baghdad as a freelance television, newspaper, and magazine reporter.

Initially I intended to be there for a couple of years, maybe three, but instead I stayed for seven and returned several times to cover some big stories, some of which are the biggest of my career, including the Arab Spring. But it was one of the most difficult and yet one of the most rewarding educations or degrees I have ever attained. Not only did I learn about the history of the Middle East and the current affairs of the Middle East, about its people and the wars and conflicts and all those things we always hear about the Middle East, but I also learned about human nature.

171

As you know, normally our job is all about beating the clock. It's about bending people's schedules to fit into ours. It's about compressing people's lives into minutes, sometimes into seconds, and slapping it all together in time for the evening newscast or website or newspaper. In the Arab world though, it's the other way around. It's about how can I get past or around or through obstacles to get my job done? How do I ensure that I don't miss my deadlines because of the things I simply cannot change? Because almost everything about the Arab world worked at cross-purposes to what my job was all about. The very minute I walked out the door to prepare a story I was walking out with a handicap. Everything was a constant battle. If it wasn't a battle against traffic, it was a battle against the multilayered bureaucracy. If it wasn't that, it was a battle just to get people to talk to us. In some countries it was a serious battle just to get permission to film anywhere in a particular city like Damascus or Cairo. Failing all that, what we occasionally faced were real battles, as one of the region's several conflicts flared up, forcing us to fight our way there to cover it.

At the start of my time in the Middle East I tried different approaches to deal with all of this. Working here in Canada, I wasn't used to these kinds of obstacles so, for example, I tried the angry indignant approach. That didn't work. I tried the meek passive aggressive approach to try to get things done, but nothing really worked until I learned simply to be patient. There is a saying in the Arab world: patience is beautiful. It's a favourite proverb there. I learned that it is beautiful but it's also infuriating and it's absolutely necessary if you are to work in the Arab world.

The guy at the customs office at the Cairo International Airport doesn't care that you need to get downtown before Friday prayers, even if it is January 28, 2011, the so-called Friday of Wrath and effectively the official start of the Egyptian revolution. What he cares about is getting the guy from the Information Ministry to come over from the other terminal and to sign for your equipment — warning you a hundred times that you would end his career if you ever left Egyptian soil without checking with him first before you flew out. That process could take minutes, it could take hours, it could take a whole day and remember: you can't lose your cool because that definitely gets you nowhere. In our case it took us a solid three hours and we made it to the hotel minutes before the tear gas started flying.

Against every grain in my body I have had no choice but to learn to be patient in the Arab world. The hardest part is that I had to do that while still somehow living up to the requirements of my job, which does not tolerate waiting very well. The surprise came when I learned somewhere in the last decade that, as infuriating as it is, waiting, patience, taking your time can actually pay dividends. At the risk of upsetting the order of things, challenging journalism professors who might be in this very audience, and rankling my own bosses who think I take too much time for everything, I'm here to sing the praises of patience, of waiting once in a while, and also of unorthodox methods the Arab world taught me that might take more time but might yield better journalism.

Presumably you've all heard of the scenic route. Well, there is no room in our job for the scenic route, normally, not unless you're coming off an assignment and you're going home the long way. But sometimes you have no choice but to take the scenic route. It was certainly the case for us when we travelled from Peshawar to Tora Bora during the war in Afghanistan, and when we travelled from Karachi to Sukkur during the floods in Pakistan, or from Amman to Beirut during the Israel-Hezbollah conflict in 2006, and the dozens of times that we drove from Amman to Baghdad and back on that lonely desert road.

The first time I went to Iraq in 2003, I took the short flight from Amman to Baghdad. One moment I was watching satellite television and a very short while later I had landed in a country where satellite dishes were illegal. Suddenly someone jumped over to me as soon as I got off the plane and whisked away my satellite phone to lock it up and ship it down to the Information Ministry in Baghdad for inspection, all before I even stepped foot outside the terminal.

The next time I travelled to Iraq it was by land and it happened to be in the dying days of the U.S. bombing of Baghdad. In that one epic journey we met border guards still in the service of Saddam Hussein. We met Special Forces soldiers in Humvees just past the border, they were almost certainly from New Zealand. We intermittently saw bombed-out vehicles and then a few minutes later we'd see Iraqis trying to sell gasoline on the side of the road, and then eventually we saw the last thing you'd expect to see. We saw an American platoon of soldiers guarding a bridge on the way into the capital, and they wouldn't let us proceed under any circumstances. We slept there, that night, in our seats in the car. After a fitful night listening to the bombing, we took a road into the city that told the story of the battle the night before. It had charred remains of bodies and twisted tanks and trees that were still on fire. When we arrived in the heart of Baghdad we spent the next few hours gathering for the evening story. Before night fell we'd witnessed American tanks rolling in to Firdos Square, the Saddam statue brought to the ground, and Baghdad liberated and occupied all at once. It was a terrifying and exhausting and nerve-racking two days, but hands-down it was far more exhilarating than any flight that got me there in an hour.

After the major combat was over I started making those road trips regularly, at least once a month. Once the Americans had taken over the Saddam International Airport, calling it the Baghdad International Airport, it was quite a while before flights started operating between Baghdad and Amman again, so the only way in or out was the road.

That one epic trip that we took during the conflict was one thing, but I wasn't particularly enamoured with this new, more-mundane version of the journey. For one, it took about eight hours on a barren, boring, dusty desert road to get from Amman to Baghdad, and it had to be done in a convoy, which is notoriously difficult to organize. Try to get a bunch of journalists to do anything together: it's one of the hardest things possible. They were tricky to plan, especially on short notice. One day, when Saddam Hussein was caught in that hole in his hometown it was no longer breaking news by the time I got there twenty-four hours later, because that was the quickest we could do it. That was one thing, but it also seemed to get more and more dangerous every time we made the trip, becoming more dangerous the closer we got to Baghdad. So we just didn't stop; we never stopped once we crossed the Jordanian border.

Eventually, though, it became too dangerous for us foreigners to travel by road, so dangerous that Iraqis stopped travelling by road. It was that

highway—it was shortly after this that we stopped travelling that highway
—that claimed the life of a close friend, one of the drivers who worked
with us before the war. Apparently, he and a friend were accosted near
the border with Syria. Their car was taken away; they were taken away,
never to be seen again. Thankfully for us, flights started running again,
so the last few times I went to Iraq we flew from Amman. Strangely, I
found myself missing the old road trip.

More than nostalgia, the road helped me prepare psychologically for
being in Baghdad. It allowed for a transition from relatively safe Amman
to the chaos and the concrete barriers of Baghdad. It was also a great way
to get to know your colleagues, the ones with whom you'd be risking
your life for the next few weeks. In the old world, in the Arab world, in
the Middle East, covering so much ground up close almost always gives
you rare glimpses of history, whether it's the Commonwealth cemetery
on the outskirts of Tobruk in Libya, the Khyber Pass on the way to
Jalalabad in Afghanistan, or parts of the Silk Road in Syria near Aleppo.

On the road you get glimpses of how neighbouring countries and their
stories meld into each other, how people are closer across those borders
than they are with people in their very own countries. More than that
though, those trips gave me a chance to gauge the situation in Iraq better
than any newspaper I had read before getting there, to ease into the current
mindset before we ever arrived. The border itself was a very good gauge.
How did the people look this time, for example? I'd be looking and seeing
Iraqis coming and going. How tense did they seem and how in a hurry
were they compared to previous trips, and who is now leaving? What kinds
of people were leaving? Was it just the poorest riding large buses together?
Was it the middle class and higher travelling in sport-utility vehicles, and
were they packing just one or two bags, going on vacation, or had they
carried most of their belongings in one of their private vehicles?

I always stopped and asked some of these questions: "How are things
in Baghdad?" Unlike the papers, their answers would contain the minutiae
you need to understand what things were really like over there. They
were out of danger, they were at the border, they were happy to talk to
me. They would explain by talking about neighbourhoods and markets

and events I would expect to know, because I had been to Iraq, but you would never see in any newspaper. They provided advice and advance insight for that inevitable question that you get as a journalist no matter where you go: what's the mood in Baghdad?

Those road trips to Iraq also gave me a regular peek at the wretched refugee camp I once visited, which sat in the no man's land between Iraq and Jordan. Was it still there, I used to ask myself as we pulled up to the border. Were there fewer or more people? How long would those people remain there, ignored by both countries involved? The road itself was also instructive. Were there lots of other cars? Passing Ramadi and Fallujah also gave us hints. Was there smoke on the skyline? Were there children on the road? Were there Humvees nearby? These are things that you cannot see from the sky.

Unfortunately, my final trip to Baghdad was by plane. By then we had taken to travelling with armed guards, which is not a great thing when you're a journalist. Even for the relatively short trip from the Baghdad airport to our home on the bank of the Tigris, that's how dangerous things had become. In fact, they were so dangerous that we hardly moved at all while we were in Baghdad, to the detriment, I think, of our journalism. As convenient, as simple as it was to travel by plane in comparison, I realized those road trips were essential in informing my storytelling, and their absence showed.

In the other trips I have taken across the Middle East, besides Iraq, I've learned all kinds of unique lessons. For one, I learned that sometimes the stories you come across on the road are the same as, as important or better, than the story you were heading over to cover. This was certainly the case when the unfinished Egyptian revolution caught up with our crew when we were trying to get to Libya to cover the revolution that started there in 2011.

For weeks when we were in Egypt those black-clad policemen — the riot police who were so instrumental in trying to quash the revolution in Cairo at the beginning — they had disappeared off the streets of Cairo and we hadn't seen them in weeks. Suddenly, we were in a town near the border of Libya and all these black-clad policemen had shown up in this little town.

They came with a lot of tear gas and a lot of shooting on the main road, right in front of our cheap hotel in the coastal village of Marsa Matrouh. This was our last stop before crossing the border to Libya and heading to Benghazi and this was an epic journey. It really was the scenic route.

We drove from Cairo on to Alexandria to Marsa Matrouh, this town I'm telling you about. We planned to continue from there to the border through to Tobruk and eventually to Benghazi. All told, it's about fifteen to eighteen hours on the road. We desperately needed a good night's sleep before getting up in the morning and continuing on our way, but the shooting wouldn't stop and so we moved to a more secure hotel further into town. Only late at night did we realize what was happening. It was what Egyptians were calling their Bastille Day. Security buildings had been sacked and set on fire, not only in Marsa Matrouh but also in Alexandria and Cairo. It was a big day. It was a very important development, but we were in the wrong place, and our task was to get to a far-bigger story as soon as possible.

Unfortunately, Marsa Matrouh would not make *The National* that night but it would be the subject of many complaints from me to Toronto. I had advised against our staying in that town on a Friday; Egypt was still going through its revolution and was still very unstable, but no one would listen to me.

On other occasions, there was no question of stopping, talking, and taking in what was in front of me and reporting it back to Canada. When the 2006 conflict started in Lebanon between Hezbollah and Israel I was in Toronto on vacation with my sister. For a couple of years I'd had a pretty bad run. It seemed like any time anything big happened in Lebanon I was away doing something else. I was constantly having to drive back to catch up with stories. Here I was again, on what was probably the biggest story, in this place I'd been based in for two years and I was on vacation in Toronto. It was very frustrating, but I was determined that come hell or high water I was going back. I had to go back.

The Beirut airport, as you might recall, had been bombed very early on. I could travel by air to London, then to Amsterdam, and then to Amman. But I had to take the road from Amman, with a taxi driver I didn't know, through Damascus over Lebanon's mountains, down the coast, and then into Beirut. I didn't sleep for two days, and it was a challenge, but given the chance to do it all over again I would do exactly the same thing. The scene that was waiting for me when we crossed that border into Lebanon and started driving up those mountains on the way towards Beirut was incredible: thousands of cars, bumper-to-bumper, taking the scenic route in the opposite direction of Syria towards a safer place.

We were travelling on this narrow road through these Christian villages because the main bridges had been made impassable after being bombed by Israeli jets, which were retaliating for the kidnapping of two Israeli soldiers by Hezbollah. We occasionally stopped to watch the endless procession of Lebanese in their cars making their way out of the country and saw all kinds of people: young people and old, Muslim, Christian. But they all had the same sort of broken, sullen expression on their faces, an expression of disbelief that they had to do this all over again, the fact that their children had to do this all over again. The sight of so many people on the move, that alone gave me a sense of how serious this particular crisis was, and the seriousness of the toll it was taking on the Lebanese, who were normally so good at adapting and making do with whatever life hands them.

As desperate as I was to get home and back to Beirut, and knowing full well I'd have to file a story that night, I could not keep my eyes off of this scene. I stood there for quite some time calling back and reporting live to both radio and television. In the end, this set the tone for weeks to come as various countries, including Canada, also felt the conflict was serious enough to evacuate their own citizens. I would never have seen that had I flown in through the airport. As angry as I was at my taxi driver — he jacked up the price when we finally arrived in Beirut — the lack of sleep and the money were well worth it, because of what I was able to witness and tell our audience.

Another lesson I have learned from these long journeys in the Middle East is there is sometimes merit in going back. One trip to Syria comes to mind. This was back when visas were pretty difficult to get, but it was certainly much safer to work there than it is today. We started out one early morning on the most boring desert road towards the border crossing with Iraq. We had heard there were thousands of Iraqis crossing every day because of the intensity of the violence going on in Iraq. There was a period when we could not even travel to Iraq. This was the only way we could gauge what was happening in Baghdad so we wanted to see it for ourselves.

It was a long dusty trip, as you can imagine, and when we got there all we saw was a small trickle of people entering Syria. There was almost nobody there. We did a couple of interviews and I met a couple of Iraqis and asked them why they were there. I shot a standup and we had more than enough for a basic story but it was vastly different than what I had been seeing and reading. Even though we were pressed for time, we had a couple days left in Damascus so decided to go back a few days later just to verify — just to be absolutely sure — that what we were seeing was reflective of reality. You have to apply for permission to go to the border, so grudgingly we reapplied.

Two days later at dawn we were driving back and saw a border that bore no resemblance whatsoever to the one we had seen a couple of days earlier: hundreds and hundreds of cars lined up as far as the eye could see. It seemed as if whole nation was on the move. For a moment I held my breath and I looked down the horizon to see the end of the lineup and I could not. The first day we had gone the Iraqi side had been cut off due to a security incident. That's why it had been so quiet.

This second day was far more representative and we spent it standing under the sun, interviewing people, talking to them about the situation in Iraq. We even had a chance to film inside the immigration building, which normally we wouldn't get to do. It was not easy, watching as Iraqi citizens were transformed into refugees, watching women cry quietly and men look passively at the children. These people had just crossed a dangerous desert and survived when so many others, including some of their own relatives and loved ones, had not. It was actually the first time I had seen anything like it.

This was before the Lebanon situation and I knew the moment I saw the lineup that this huge displacement would have far-reaching consequences on the region, not only on the region but on Iraq itself. In that moment, standing at that border seemed so significant that that was the moment I decided to write my book. Today, six years later, many of those people are still displaced. In fact, many of them are now threatened by new violence, the violence that's happening in Syria, the place where they had sought refuge. And so, like tens of thousands of Syrians, they're going to be displaced yet again.

Sometimes I went back to places long after I had first visited; journalists do this on a fairly regular basis just to see what's changed. It is a luxury in the Middle East, where we didn't always have the time, and where it wasn't always easy to get to the same spots you had seen before. But I did do it once in 2007. It was a year after the war, the conflict between Hezbollah and Israel, was over. I returned to southern Lebanon to see how the rebuilding was going and decided to visit a very specific stretch of road that had been almost completely destroyed by the fighting in 2006. The first time I actually went there was in 2006, literally a day after the war had ended, and I was amazed at the destruction. At the time we had come across a woman standing in the area. She looked as amazed as I was, looking down the road from a hill, into the rubble, calling out the name of a woman. When we asked her who she was looking for, she said she had an elderly friend who lived down there. She hadn't seen her since the war started and she'd been looking for her all day. With the smell of death in the air and the destruction in front of us she assumed this lady had died but didn't want to believe it.

On the anniversary of that conflict I decided to go back to exactly that stretch of road and found a very different scene. It was a bustling town, lots of cars, the market was awake, and all kinds of people were around, except for that little spot where we'd found that woman a year earlier. There was still some rubble in that area and as I looked down, at first I thought I was seeing things, there was that elderly lady sitting amidst the rubble drinking a cup of tea. We went down to talk to her, of course, and as you might expect in that part of the world, she insisted we must have tea. She got up with some difficulty and walked into what looked like a standing structure, three walls and a roof, and came back with a full kettle. She put on a little burner and soon we were having tea and talking about her story.

We were sitting on her doorstep and all that was left of her house was the bathroom, which was the part that was standing, and a little herb garden she used to plant. She had been very reluctant to leave her house during the conflict because she had been living there almost her whole life. She'd been living in that house since she was married at fourteen and was well into her seventies when we met her. She was eventually persuaded to leave but every day since the war ended, despite the fact it had been pummelled to pieces, she still came down to visit the house. She would stay in the shade of that bathroom until sunset, then make her way back to the house of friends where she was staying.

Many of her neighbours had rebuilt their own homes, but she told us she had received no compensation money yet. In any case, her children were in America and she didn't quite know where to begin to rebuild her home. She said she was simply thankful to be alive, contrary to what we thought and her friend thought a year earlier. And she simply waited, hoping that someone, somehow would help her resurrect her precious house. It was a rewarding if also heartbreaking second look at that little stretch of road.

But going back to the unorthodox list of rules in the Middle East: at some point I learned that surviving as a foreign correspondent in the Middle East wasn't really about journalism at all. I know that sounds shocking, but I'll explain. Of course, being inquisitive is important, being a good writer is important, being a keen observer is essential in a good foreign correspondent. But if you did not know how to navigate the bureaucracy or how to be a travel agent, how to be a negotiator, a medic, a psychologist; if you didn't know how to fix minor technical problems with computers or equipment, if you didn't know how to set up a satellite phone or file using a cellphone — if you do not know how to solve problems — then you will almost certainly fail as a foreign correspondent.

I spent as much time, if not more, being an accountant for the CBC as I have been being a journalist. Getting high-speed Internet into my office in Lebanon became a part-time job for about a year. It was such a sweet accomplishment when it was over I wanted to put it on my resume.

When we travelled it was getting that visa, finding the right drivers and translators, making sure you have the right food and enough fuel to get to where you're going, getting a convoy together, plotting a route, and then arbitrating when people on your convoy disagreed about how to get onto the route. It was making sure everyone meets on time and has all the right papers, that they have enough passport photos to make it through the border, and then making sure everyone gets on the road early enough to make it to where you wanted to go before dark.

Because I spoke both languages, Arabic and English, it fell to me to negotiate the borders we crossed and take all passports from one official to the other, to get all the stamps necessary to get through and on to the next border. Sometimes though, this being the Middle East, you can solve all the problems and fail through no fault of your own.

My favourite example is from 2009, when we were waiting at the Gaza border. You might recall the three-week conflict between Hamas and Israel, and very few journalists were inside at the time. We were not getting in on the Israeli side, so a group of us travelled to the Egyptian side to try to get in that way. We had heard rumours that the next day Israel was going to declare a unilateral ceasefire. Egyptian officials were already saying that if that happened they would allow the journalists in, the caveat being, of course, that we had to have a letter from our embassy. This happens all the time in the Middle East, absolving them of any responsibility should anything happen to us.

We assumed our embassy would do what all the other embassies were doing, which is to fax this letter to our hotel in El Arish, about five hours from Cairo. Shockingly, they refused. They insisted on us being there in person to get the letter and we were a solid five hours away. I tried to persuade them to understand our situation, that they were putting me at greater risk of death by forcing me to drive up and down that highway at night. But they simply would not budge.

In the interest of staying on schedule and being prepared to enter Gaza the next day, I jumped into our van with our driver and we made the five-hour journey back to Cairo for a meeting with embassy staff that lasted minutes. Then we jumped backed into the van and returned to El Arish to leave the next morning for Gaza. I did not take an unduly long time to complain about the obstinacy of the embassy because, like I said, this job is about solving problems. Complaining would only have delayed me and I had no time to waste. We did, thanks to the letter, get into Gaza that night, but not before another lesson going right back to the beginning, that lesson in the casual unfairness of working in the Middle East. After waiting four hours in front of the border crossing, the police finally let us in on foot, dragging our bags and flak jackets behind us. They asked us to line up in front of one official's window to get the stamp into our passports and to go on our way.

The lineup was moving very, very slowly, which was not a surprise, and we stood there for hours waiting for our turn. It was starting to get dark and suddenly we were told sorry, but no more journalists were going to be processed that day. Those of us left in line had to hike back with our stuff and flak jackets and come back the next morning. Just like that.

After all those efforts, all those hoops we had to jump through, all the things that we did right, arranging a place to stay in Gaza that night and coordinating with the driver on when to pick us up, that wretched trip up and down the highway to get that letter — we did all of it only to be left behind while our competition, simply by being ahead of us in line, actually made it in. You can imagine how crushing this was, and it wasn't the first time. Every time something like this happened I would ask myself, why do I continue doing this? Why am I working in this business?

The moment our cameraman and I got back into our waiting van outside the gates, I burst into tears. What else do you do? I was exhausted and frustrated and I was upset because my next action was calling my boss to explain, before my competition showed up on the air, what happened. He sounded empathetic but the reality was that I would not be on the air from Gaza that night and that's how that day would be remembered. Just as suddenly, as I was explaining through my tears, we heard a commotion near the gate. Someone yelled out and said yes, in the end, we could cross that night, to come back now. It was about eleven o'clock. I hung up on my boss and we ran with what little energy we had left, and finally, after a long wait, we made it to the Palestinian side of the border. We waited again, this time for our passports. Eventually we made it out with our driver, and within minutes of him describing the past month of conflict we'd forgotten about our minor inconveniences over the last couple of days.

If there's one thing that's almost unavoidable in the Middle East it is a long interview — with politicians, businessmen, ordinary people. They want to give you the full story, even after I would warn them that we're only going to use one small part of this. But they feel obligated to tell you the story from top to bottom because people there are storytellers, which is a blessing when you're a journalist. You want people who tell a good story, but sometimes you're just in a really big hurry. You simply have to be polite and listen and so I learned to be patient, as I mentioned, to sit and to listen.

I learned to build that extended interview into our tight filing-day schedule, and eventually I learned that the longer the interview, the better the outcome. This is not only because of the obvious, because they give you more detail and context, but invariably, in my experience, people revealed crucial bits of information two-thirds of the way into an interview. Don't ask me why. I have no idea, but interviews in the Middle East just somehow, whether it's a comfort thing, they followed the perfect story arc. The best information would come only about two-thirds or three-quarters of the way, instead of at the beginning. I learned to wait for that.

Once, we came upon one teenage girl and her family in a school in the middle of Gaza. Her mother suggested I interview her daughter because she wasn't speaking. She had stopped eating, which had started when the family was displaced from their home, which was damaged in the fighting. The girl was really shy and said very little when I said hello. It was a few tense minutes before she mustered a hello back. Over the next few minutes she slowly started to engage and respond, with gestures at first, and then with some small talk. Eventually she was putting full sentences together and explained that she could no longer go on. She was about seventeen and said she could not go on because their home had been destroyed. More importantly, all of her records were gone. All her report cards, her awards, everything she had ever worked for had all been burned. By this point we were deep in conversation. Her statements were growing more articulate and more furious and then suddenly she started to cry but she kept talking, she kept talking more and more passionately and clearly until finally she surprised me by switching to almost-flawless English.

When I asked her how she learned she said she had mostly taught herself. It was then and only then when her mother piped up, about an hour into our talk, that I was speaking to the top-rated grade eleven student in all of Gaza. She was the smartest kid in the entire strip. She was a genius and here she was, a refugee, in — of all places — a classroom, just weeks before she was to begin her final exams. These would determine what would happen to her after grade twelve, and she wanted to be an English teacher. This woman defined herself by her schoolwork and prided herself on her achievements, it was all she owned, and she could not accept moving on after losing all of it. She was one of the most exceptional characters I've ever included in a story and I wouldn't have found out any of that if I'd asked the usual few questions and moved on.

Over time I simply learned the art of waiting. I waited for a frustrating six years before I got, after trying a hundred times or more, an Iranian visa to visit Tehran. It was worth every minute of waiting, to be there on the eve of a historic election, to watch the birth of a pro-democracy movement that arguably helped inspire the Arab Spring. Of course I will wait for a few more hours in cold and dark Tahrir Square to see whether history will be made that night, or whether the youth who had waited their entire lives would walk away empty-handed again despite their best efforts. Yes, I will wait to speak to the men behind the microphone at Radio Free Libya and I will wait for each of them to explain their stories, why they were taking their lives into their own hands. They had been waiting forty years to tell their stories; I could certainly wait forty minutes.

This brings me to a final lesson in patience I learned in the Arab world, but perhaps it's the most significant. It's not the most popular thing to say these days, with dying news budgets and shrinking pots for foreign reportage, but the pressure to go somewhere only when it's necessary, to do what you need to do and just get out is huge. I know this. Every time we're sent out the door to cover a breaking story we feel that pressure. It's also an era, as you all know, where bureaus are getting smaller, or they're closing, or they're being mothballed and they're never coming back. But the fact remains, that the longer we stay in the places we cover and the more often we go back, the more we know and the better our stories. It's just a simple fact.

I never lived in Egypt, but I started going there in 2005. That was during the first contested presidential election since Mubarak had taken power. I spoke to a lot of people, even travelled to Mubarak's hometown and talked to people there at length. I met with members of the Muslim Brotherhood and the spokesman for the Muslim Brotherhood at the time told me something I remember to this day. He said that in Egypt democracy would never be granted, that it would have to be seized. How true would his words ring many years later?

I even covered a very small protest on election day back in 2005, in a small traffic circle called Tahrir Square. It was there I started to get an idea of how frustrated Egyptian youth had become. They were very well educated but had few opportunities, and on top of that they had no political freedom and lived in an authoritarian, incredibly corrupt state. I mentioned some of these findings in my stories but mostly I filed them in my mind for another time, along with similar stories I had heard in other Arab countries. Over the years I went back time and again to Egypt and began to understand the predicament of the country's youth, of all the region's youth. It was, as I've said repeatedly, the largest generation of young people the Middle East has ever seen, and their frustrations were just as monumental.

As I got ready to leave the region, back in 2009, I was sad we were closing the CBC bureau there. As I packed my five hundred tapes we had gathered in places like Syria, Egypt, Iraq, and Lebanon over seven years, I realized that the region — which had been stuck for so long, so stagnant — could no longer remain the way it was; not much longer. I'm not claiming to have predicted the Arab Spring but I knew back then, in 2009, that the status quo could not hold for long. I had seen the signs for years that something somehow was coming.

Early on, as you might recall, I witnessed the Lebanese protests in 2005, so passionate they managed to bring down a government for the first time in recent memory in the Middle East. I witnessed the shock of Arab people as they witnessed the once-powerful Saddam Hussein captured, humiliated, and later executed. After Tehran I followed Iranians who were covering their own revolution on Twitter and Facebook, where it lives on long after it fizzled on the streets. And all along I wondered why nobody was doing something to deal with the youths' frustrations. The signs were all there, the ingredients were all in place, and all it needed was a spark. That is almost literally what happened when Mohammed Bouazizi set himself on fire in December 2010, just over a year after I closed down our Arab world bureau.

All those lessons learned from journey after journey into Egypt allowed me to see, right away, that the moment the Tunisian president stepped down it was Egypt's turn. It wasn't because I was somehow gifted in telling the future, or prescient in some way, but in all those long interviews over all those years I had been well-schooled in Egypt's story. As a student of the Middle East I had been tutored by some of its best experts — ordinary people. They helped me note the nuances and hear the drumbeats heralding the advance of change. I don't think it's enough to just show up, notebook in hand, in some of these more troubled parts of the world, like the Middle East, when the predictable spasms of violence suddenly command our attention. Covering the world's conflicts, no matter where they are, is not a job well-suited, I think, to war correspondents, to whom every conflict is the same.

I think to cover a conflict or troubled part of the world you need to do one of two things: either you need to live in the region you're covering or you need to visit a lot to understand, to learn the reasons, to log the nuances, and to keep track of the quiet when it does come along with the noise. In other words, foreign correspondence in itself is an exercise in patience. It is all about the waiting, and then it's all about how the waiting ends.

I waited a long time in the Middle East and when the wait ended I made my way to Cairo, back to a story I understood perfectly. Once the customs guy finally let us out of the airport we rushed to our hotel. Within minutes of our arrival I was on the news, live, and the questions came like a waterfall. Why were they protesting? What's motivating them? Who are these people and where have they been for the past few decades? And I already knew the answers. I'd taken that class, I'd gotten my degree in Egypt's malaise, and it wasn't because I'm so smart, but because I just spent the time. For a very long time I sat on the floor of the business centre of our hotel answering those questions.

Why were the youth frustrated? They were educated and yet could not find a job. They had had to endure bread lineups and riots. Because young men found it almost impossible to raise the money necessary to get married. I'd been there, spoken to the people, and learned these things well in advance. No amount of reading could have prepared me better for covering this story than those years I had spent in the region.

All those days of frustration, battles and obstacles, witnessing violence, crossing endless borders, waiting for something to change in a region best known for stagnation — they all counted for something. When people ask me what's it like working in the Arab world, my immediate answer is that there was always a lot of waiting, and that most of the time it was worth it.

November 7, 2012

DAVID CARR
The Next Big Thing

When David Carr came to campus in the fall of 2013, he sat with a group of journalism students and, in about ten minutes, explained what has happened to legacy media, where new media is now, and where it may be in the future. He was funny, blunt, irreverent, and smart. That's what makes him the most influential writer on the media in the world. Today, the veteran reporter writes the Media Equation column for the New York Times, *and also reports on popular culture. His book,* The Night of the Gun, *is a memoir of addiction and recovery. He is an old school reporter who knows he's onto a big story and isn't letting go.*

I'm going to claim a little kind of honorary Canadian status because Minnesota, as you may know, is right up on Canada. We wear Canada as kind of a great big hat, right? I'm a Minnesotan. I worked in hockey. That means we're brothers. The other thing is Minnesotans, like Canadians, are not only humble but very proud of their humility. We both talk the same and we talk nice.

So how humble and nice are Canadians? When that Rob Ford video came out — the one he said did not exist, and it finally came out that, yes indeed he was smoking that crack, having a little bit of crack — his approval ratings in Toronto went up what, four or five points? You guys are so nice. It's unbelievable.

The thing I like about Mr. Ford is, most of the time, when you think of crackheads you think of really emaciated thin people, and I like a guy who can focus both on the crack and his groceries at the same time. Kind of a high achiever, right? He just likes sticking things in his mouth. No, really. He can get the whiskey in there, the crack pipe, the doughnut. Everything will go in. There are only so many hours in a day but he manages to do his job, sort of, get high, and tell all manner of lies. You just got to hand it to the guy, that somebody could be big and bold and fat and on the crack like that guy.

I know because I was that guy. I once weighed about two hundred and eighty pounds and was addicted to crack. So when I see Mr. Ford struggling I see myself, a five-time treatment loser person who lied just for practice. A person who thought everybody else was the problem. And so I don't really judge the guy. I wish he would quit with the lying. At a certain point it's like, game over, dude. It's done. Give it up. And then today the *Toronto Star* had that video of him just going crazy. The thing that was disturbing about the video is that the whole first half was shot from the waist down. Have you guys seen it? It'll cause eye damage if you watch it. You're not going to be able to un-see that anytime soon.

So when I see this guy I think of myself. I was flat on my back, but one good thing led to another. I sobered up; I got custody of my kids. I got jobs. I got other jobs. I did what I was supposed to do. I quit telling lies and I ended up in the back of a Bombardier plane on my way out here. I rode in the middle seat. You know the way, way back? You totally want to stay out of that seat. That thing is a nightmare. I was next to one of your fellow citizens who was both reading a book on doughnuts and had had a few doughnuts as well.

I tell all of this not just as a cheap joke, but because I think the not-so-honourable mayor brings to mind the media age we're living in. He offers a kind of tutorial in modern media. You've got to wonder what Dalton Camp would be saying about him right now.

I covered Marion Barry for five years, and this guy totally takes the cake. I mean he is unbelievable; he is a movie unto himself. But think about the media aspect of this. What brought him down? Was it the *Toronto Star*? Was it Gawker? Was it some intrepid reporter? Not really. It was one person with a cellphone who made a video of him. That's the time we're living in. If it can be known, it will be known, and that person with the cellphone did what all the king's horses and all the king's men could not do. That's the media age that we're living in.

And once that video existed, it would be found. And good on Gawker and good on the *Toronto Star* for getting it done. I think it's interesting, because you have a tabloid with a strong tradition of municipal coverage in one of Canada's great cities and then you've got this weird blog in Manhattan that has heard this story and the blog crowd fundraises a hundred thousand dollars to try and get the video to squirt out, and then the *Toronto Star* is prompted into action. They both ended up moving together, and eventually the story is known and the cops end up with the video and now the word is out.

The legacy media has satellite trucks, trucks for delivery, printing presses, the websites have Twitter accounts and blogs, but they're each having an impact on the public discourse and my prediction is that they'll meet in the middle. Where I work, I mean if you take Twitter as an example, once every three seconds there's a Tweet containing *New York Times* information. If you're a paper like ours, a news organization in search of the new audience, in search always of a fresh younger demographic, Twitter doesn't turn out to be your enemy, it turns out to be your friend. We do seventy blogs; we do a lot of video. I've done nine years of video since I've been there and I probably am not what you would think of as a television star, but on the web I work just fine. People expect a newspaper reporter to look like me. I covered the Oscars for four years, including doing those horrible interviews on the carpet and I looked, it looked like a homeless guy had gotten loose out on the carpet. Imagine me and Kate Winslet. I interviewed Scarlett Johansson when she wore that one red dress that was very, very famous.

We've got seven hundred thousand people who pay us for digital access, and then if you look at the rising blogs in Manhattan — BuzzFeed, Gawker, Business Insider — the minute they get a couple of nickels to rub together what do they do? They hire reporters. And the pace of change of these two things coming together is breathtaking. BuzzFeed is mostly cats and lists of things your aunt did on her skateboard, or whatever.

Then they hired this really good journalist, Ben Smith, and not seven months later they were partnered with us on the election. Wow, that was fast. The thing is, you guys grew up bathed in this. You grew up and this was just very much a part of your life. To us, we watched this on *The Jetsons* when we were little. I can remember.

I washed out of journalism for reasons that are probably manifest. When I came back, I got a story, I got an assignment. I'd been out of the business for a couple of years and the guy gave me an assignment and he said: "Well, just fax it to us."

I said, "What do you mean?" This was about 1990. "What do you mean, 'Fax it to us?'"

"Well, you take a piece of paper, you put it in a machine, it goes through a phone wire, and then it comes out as a piece of paper at the other end."

I said, "That can't be true, that can't be right, no way that could happen."

He said, "Just go to Kinko's, tell them you want to fax something, and give them our fax phone number."

Think about things now. I have more power in my backpack than I've had in the whole newsroom that I walked into. It's a very different age that we live in. It's very easy to make media, right? Part of the problem that newspapers and other people have, you guys are so busy making media that you don't have time to consume it. You're so busy emailing, Facebooking, tweeting, Instagraming, Tumblring, whatever you darn kids are doing, that you don't have time to take in our stuff. Think about when you wake up. The newspaper and the morning show used to own that moment. When you wake up now, what is the most interesting media to you in the world? It's your email. It's about you. It's to you, for you, about you. So already you're just getting out of bed, maybe you're not even out of bed, you're already checking your email, so the morning show on CBC, the morning show on television, the newspaper — we're all waiting behind your email. You're busy. And sometimes you get so busy with that you forget about us altogether and it hurts, I've got to say. The challenge for me and to us is fight our way out of the clutter. It's to be the signal amidst all the noise, right?

I think about books. I like reading books but I'm really having trouble reading books because while they're very easy to get on the iPad or on the Kindle, you can never tell quite how far you are, right? And if you see someone on an airplane reading a book on the iPad, what do you really know about him or her? You know that they've got $500 for an iPad, that's all you know. Like this guy I was riding with on this Bombardier, his book had pictures of doughnuts on the front, so I learned something about him. Or the person reading *The Economist* or the person reading the *Financial Times* or the person reading the *Globe and Mail*. It signals in a way that the iPad does not.

Think of your nightstand at home and how busy it has become. On my nightstand I have a stack of books I should read, so there's that stack. And then there's another stack of books I should read by friends of mine. And then there's even a stack of books I should read by friends of mine who I know I'm going to bump into.

If you think about what's next to that stack, there's not just a remote but the remote has a DVR, right? And it also has video on demand, so it seems like everything that's ever been made is right there. I also have a Roku on my nightstand, which means that everything that's on the web I can have as well. So we've gone from five channels to fifty channels to five hundred channels to five thousand channels to an infinite number of channels and we still haven't figured out the navigation. I just want to see something that I would like. Right now, you have to go up to it and hit it with a stick and hope something cool pops out. But once your television knows who you are, knows what you like, can recommend, can show you by price point, a lot's going to happen.

I've been thinking a lot about what television is. I was on a set a week ago with John Goodman. He is in a series written by Garry Trudeau, the author of *Doonesbury,* and Clark Johnson is there and Cynthia Nixon from *Sex and the City.* Who's making that show? Amazon is making that show. How weird is that? And how do you get that show from Amazon? You become an Amazon Prime member and they just like, throw it in. So content is a throw-in.

Last year, who won the best director Emmy? Netflix won it. Netflix. A company that was previously the biggest user of the U.S. Postal Service, now the biggest user of download on the Internet, and they're winning Emmys for their programming. It can't be good for the media companies, right? Because they've had these monopolies for a long, long time, but what's bad for them is good for you. Think about the Netflix streaming service. How many people here have Netflix? And why wouldn't you? It's about eight dollars and it used to be a service with good movies and crappy TV and now it's crappy movies and good TV. And for $7.99 a month how much do you get to see? You see *House of Cards*, that's totally worth it. *Orange Is the New Black*, boy that's worth it, too.

When you have those kinds of options, you can see that the bundles, the monopoly that television has had historically on the consumer, is breaking up. My cable bill is two hundred dollars. Included in that is about six dollars for ESPN. I never watch ESPN, never, ever, ever. I like NFL football but the idea that you would spend time watching a couple of dorks talking about a game that happened four days ago, well, kill me now. I don't watch it, but I still pay for it.

What happens when we're able as consumers to start to pull that apart and only buy what we want? Think about what happened in newspapers. Newspapers sold you a bundle. I only like the crossword — well you got to buy the whole damn thing. I only follow the sports section — you have to buy the whole thing. That's what the Internet did. Pulled it apart so that if you just want sports we're going to give you that. What it did, was it drew a lot of the inefficiency out of the system.

Think of the way music used to be sold is, if there were two songs on the new Arcade Fire record — which is a great record by the way — that you liked, you had to buy the whole record. Now you can buy the only two that you want. Again, taking inefficiency out of the system. But you know what? Media companies have another word for that inefficiency: it's called *profit*, so they like that inefficiency.

Networks used to be built on a system in which at eight p.m. on Thursday night the program you want to see is on. Once upon a time in

America nine, ten, twelve million people, twenty million people all showed up at a certain time and all sitting through the commercials, right? That doesn't happen anymore. The consumers are producing their environment.

I was watching an NFL game and it was mind-blowing how many commercials there were. I thought, they must have increased the number of commercials from last year. And then I realized I haven't seen a commercial since last year, since last NFL season. Everything I have is recorded on DVR or it's on pay-per-view. It's at a point now where if you watch a commercial you end up feeling like a loser. Just to tell you how much things have changed, when I was twenty-four years old I wrote a very significant story about police violence. I did this story for a little local weekly that had a hundred thousand people in circulation. I'm going to generously estimate that thirty thousand read my story. My daughter, her name is Erin Lee Carr, a great young journalist. She did a story for Vice about a guy who uses 3D printers to make the only part of the gun that you can't get over the Internet. It has over seven million views. I'd like to choke the life out of her! Doesn't really seem fair, does it? And what we're seeing, I think, is in this instance, the way it worked with her, is that Vice is an independent media company. The story got picked up by Digg and then YouTube got wind of it and sent it into outer space. That's not even her most popular video. My kid has been seen and watched by more people than I ever have and I've been doing this since before the invention of dirt.

Who knows what the most popular regularly scheduled program was on American television last year? Zombies. *The Walking Dead*. Huge. Not only that but *Walking Dead* beat all the networks, right? They had a show about *Walking Dead* that was just talking about the *Walking Dead* called *Talking Dead*, so it's a show about a show talking about a show. That show about a show outdrew everything that NBC had in prime time, so things have changed a lot. The idea of what mass means anymore has changed. The whole idea that you could blow a whistle at a certain time and everyone would show up is over. We're able to program our own little media cocoons.

I got a new car and it recognizes that I have nine thousand songs on my phone and plays them. I'm probably never going to listen to the radio again, other than CBC, of course, and NPR. It seems we're able to program our own little mediated universe.

When your kids grow up, you will tell them that news organizations used to decide at a certain point in the day to stop gathering news, write it all down, print it on the paper, and then roll it up in bundles and throw it in people's yards. As Clay Shirky, a professor at NYU has pointed out, people are not going to believe that ever happened.

In the context of all this, everything is companion media. You don't watch television without something else in your lap. You go to read a book on the iPad but then you just check your mail on the iPad and forty minutes later you wake up and go: where was I, what was I doing? All I did was follow a link, right? I just came from a conference in Dublin and people had come from all over the country and all over Europe and all over the United States to come to this conference, to get this badge that costs a lot of money, to talk about technology. What were they all doing? They were all standing there looking at their phones. Your view has not changed from where you were before you came here: your house. You came here for an offline experience, you came here to meet these people, but you're answering your email instead.

There's a game people play in Silicon Valley and sometimes in New York where you have a bunch of tech nerds and they all will put their phones stacked on the table. The first one to pull their phone out has to pay the bill. I think that's a nice trap, right? As long as I'm not the one grabbing the phone.

It all comes at a cost. You think it is so nice Google is giving you all these products for free. There's a saying in the Valley: when what you're getting is free, you are the product. The Valley does care about the quality of information, though. They don't want the Internet to be this big cesspool that spiders have to crawl across. They want it to have good information. They care about there being good business models to go with it and they're not just saying that.

Think about the past four months: a half a billion dollars has come into serious news and information. Jeff Bezos bought the *Washington Post* for $250 million. And then Pierre Omidyar, the guy who invented eBay, is going to put $250 million into a site built around Glenn Greenwald.

I think that's really exciting, because if you think about what these guys are good at, which is working on their platform in which they learn what you like, serve up other things that you might like, that could come in handy in the serious news business. We in the news business could learn a few things about that.

We have learned a few things at the *New York Times*. We now have seven hundred thousand consumers who pay us on the web. In 2012, for the first time in our history, we received more money from consumers than we got out of ads. We've sold off assets. We now have a billion dollars on hand.

Things are better at big papers, but I worry about the middle, the regional newspapers that do important accountability reporting.

But if you look at this sort of crazy mixed-up, mashed-up world, all different platforms, people who are doing not just one thing but many things, I think to myself, you know what? I bet you Dalton Camp would like that. He wasn't just a politician. He was a very elegant voice on the radio. He wasn't just a radio commentator, not that that isn't a great calling, but also a person who advised other politicians, a man of letters, a newspaper columnist — I think he would prosper in an age like this and I am deeply honoured to give this lecture.

Q: I'm a big fan. I watched you on Bill Maher and then in the *Page One* documentary. I don't get an online subscription because there's still too much clutter and I was wondering if you've ever thought about bundling where people could just buy the columnists that they like?

A: Bundling columnists — I think we're going to get in a place where, given the fact that people are blowing up on Twitter, watch what Omidyar does with his new site. It's a federation of well-known names with a lot of social media following and I think you're onto something where, if you think of Andrew Sullivan in the United States, where people are giving him money, I think individual brands matter. In the instance of the *New York Times*, I don't think many people would pay attention to what I have to say if I didn't work at the *New York Times* so I have a superstitious belief in staying there, but other people may feel differently.

Q: This morning you spoke about the need for young journalists to stand out, so could you provide three top tips for us?

A: Well, I think rushing up to the microphone to ask a question afterwards is a good start. I commend you. Taking the risk to be heard and coming up with a question — risk taking is important. I do think having a serious presence on social media is important. Not everything is great. You probably shouldn't post, "Miley Cyrus isn't the only one who can twerk. Watch this man!"

But having a social media presence that reflects you in all of your glory — if twerking's your thing, no big deal, but mix it in with some other stuff. The other way to stick out is I think to be a serious consumer of serious information. I hear so many people making speeches about things they don't know anything about. You never hear anybody these days say, "I don't know" or "I'm not sure." When I left college I had a professor — because I was a good student, he gave me a list of a hundred American authors I should read and I read them and I think it helped me. It helped me get a little focused.

Q: What do you think the smaller, more medium-sized newspapers could learn from the *New York Times*'s successful online presence and do you think they can stay afloat if they catch on fast enough?

A: That's a tough one, because the *New York Times*'s business I think is the *New York Times*'s business, that they're in that specific business like the *Wall Street Journal* is in the *Wall Street Journal* business. I think the better answers are like, in America, the *Minneapolis Star Tribune* has used a combination of consumer marketing of their circulation plus limited paywalls. The *Arkansas Democrat* has never allowed their paper to go free.

The whole model has kind of changed. It used to be — kids didn't read the paper, then they went to college, then they hook up, then they go to Ikea, then they reproduce, then they have to buy a minivan. All that's gone. People don't even get married right after college, and if they do, there are all sorts of blogs and digital coupons to help them out. So that whole kind of retail underbelly that drove good-sized papers, I think, is gone. I think that you expect to charge people for journalism, you have to commit journalism, and so, investing in the product over and over, they're essentially sending out something that is the size and has the value of a brochure. Consumers will respond that there is nothing left there for you to charge them for. So you have to maintain the journalistic horsepower if you expect citizens to come with you.

Q: Technology has definitely helped journalism and communications and media but do you feel there are ways that it's hindered it, as well?

A: On the news producing side, technology has been unbelievably helpful. If you're interviewing somebody, you have all known thought one click away. Let's say a source is avoiding you, you can freaking stalk him on Twitter, Facebook, and LinkedIn. The problem is that technology has created an absence of scarcity so content and ads double every year. It's so much harder to stick out. And the other thing is that price derives from scarcity, so if there's no scarcity, you can't raise the price on anything, the price of ads just keeps going down. It's ruined the business model but it's made doing journalism a lot more fun.

Q: Do you worry that the average reporter will eventually lose their ability to critically analyze and critically pay attention to details given the abundance of distractions? And, I'm really pushing the limits with a double-barrelled question here, but if so, how do we keep that skill?

A: The metric going forward is not how beautiful something you made is, but how fast can you do it?

I had the privilege of sitting on a panel with Gay Talese one time and he said, "We are outside people. We leave, we go outside the office and we find people more interesting than us and we come back and tell our audience what they said." There's a danger, if all you're doing is taking information, putting a little topspin on it, sending it out into the world, that you're never going to leave the building. How is the world ever going to leak into you in a significant way if you don't get out? I write a Monday media column and it's hard not to feel like I'm wasting time when I go out of the building and then I remember that this is called reporting.

Q: Do you think it's a citizen's duty to be informed or spend x amount of time being aware of what's globally going on just as much as locally? If so, what type of balance should a person do to make sure that they're equally knowledgeable of local and international news?

A: I think all audiences should be Canadian. You guys ask such good questions, like, you Canadians — sneaky smart. When I came to the *New York Times*, I came from a dot-com news operation and I'd watch them make the front page. They'd have the page one meeting and the web would be up above them and stories would be changing and morphing and colliding and I would think, it's so dumb you're going to decide what the six or seven most important stories in the world are, why would you even do that? And now I've come to really love it. Part of the reason is that all day long information comes whooshing by — Rob Ford, Justin Bieber, NATO — zooming by me all day long. I know everything, but I know nothing and so the next day that newspaper serves as kind of a full stop, a hierarchy of importance. That's the value of a print newspaper. I say that because I still get the daily paper of the *New York Times*. If I'm on the web, I never read enough important stuff. If I'm self-selecting what I'm going to read, but when I see it in the newspaper with the pictures, it matters. How do I know that forty percent of the Syrian population is on the brink of starvation? I read that in the newspaper. I probably read it because there was a picture of one of them that spoke to me as a person and if I'm on the web I'm always hitting the Bieber button or I'm stuck on the media news. I'm self-selecting into a media vertical that just reflects my interests, not the broader interests, so I take the print product because it drags me across information that I need to know.

I mean, given that this is a Dalton Camp lecture, I think that you have to say that the responsibility of the citizenry is definitional to this country. A truly free press arrived late to Canada and it, in context, is an incredibly precious resource and when you have public officials, never mind Rob Ford, who are treating their office as a sinecure, as a place where they can pad personal expense at the expense of people, how important is it for people to pay attention to it? Well think of the alternative, you know? It's pretty important.

Q: What do you think has been the key to your success?

A: The key to my success? Obviously my rapacious good looks and beautiful voice. I'm a worker, I'm an earner and that which cannot be known is the most interesting thing in the world for me. I never, ever stop. If you tell me I can't have something I'm going to get it.

Q: I've had to ask quite a few people recently a lot of things about the newspapers around Fredericton, and something that came up a lot was that they believed the newspaper was going to die because news is such a catch-up-or-you-get-left-behind world. Do you believe in that? And if not, what kind of things does the newspaper need do to keep its readership, to keep the people wanting it?

A: I was flying over to Dublin, which is not a place I know well, but they gave out the *Irish Times* on the way over. I could smell the place and feel the place in that newspaper. I felt like it was a rigorous and true mirror of what was going on there and it made me feel like I was part of something and I think you can do that with a newspaper or with a website.

I do think that we can't lose the maypoles that we organize around. We all can't sit in our basement and read the blogs that we agree with and watch Fox News or watch MSNBC because we agree with them. I just don't think that that's going to work long run. In America we shut down our government just because people were unwilling to deal with the same set of facts. You could say, oh those darn politicians, but the people were no better. We lack a village commons. I think that by self-assembling down these deep wells where we can't even see each other — everything will be lost. I think the secret for a news organization, a newspaper, a television station, a radio station is — the super-secret sauce is: do something amazing, all the time. Sometimes when I travel I come back to the *New York Times*, I look at it and I just can't believe that the likes of me works at a place like that. It's like an amazing, amazing artifact. It emerges not just from one person but from the spaces between people. I think this common purpose of trying to make it as good as you can, as fast as you can, and hold up a rigorous, useful mirror that citizens can use to be better informed and be part of some kind of republic is a worthy and great thing and I don't think it's going away.

November 7, 2013

ACKNOWLEDGEMENTS

Senator Norman Atkins is responsible for raising the money to create the Dalton Camp Endowment in Journalism, which supports this lecture series and many other programs at St. Thomas University. Senator Atkins, who died in 2010, loved Dalton Camp and pursued this project relentlessly. He could never understand why we didn't sell 50/50 tickets on lecture night. Former vice-president academic Richard Myers was there in the beginning and, as was his way, just made things happen. Former STU president Daniel O'Brien and his wife Valerie are great supporters of the series and hosted speaker receptions in their home during the early years.

Jeffrey Carleton, STU communications director, has played a central role in the series, both helping to select speakers and coordinating publicity for the events. He is responsible for our full house year after year. For many years, Jacqueline Cormier has worked behind the scenes to make each event a success. My steadfast friend and colleague Michael Camp has been a co-organizer since the beginning. We have also had great support from Penny Granter, Becky Soffee, Susan Sears, and Rebecca Phillips.

At CBC, former *Ideas* executive producer Bernie Lucht embraced this lecture series with enthusiasm, travelling to Fredericton every year and conducting workshops for our students. He has become a true friend of our university. *Ideas* host Paul Kennedy has introduced every speaker in the series with grace and style. In recent years, radio producer Mary Lynk has coordinated the lectures. She helped us choose speakers and convince our guests that a visit to Fredericton in the fall is a good idea. Radio technician Carrie Blanchard recorded all the lectures in the series, and when she is in the building we know the event is in the hands of a true professional.

Many thanks to our fine students and members of the Fredericton community who continue to fill the room for this lecture series.

I also want to thank my wife Deborah Nobes who, since the beginning, has had all the good ideas.

About the Editor

An award-winning newspaper reporter, magazine writer, and editor, Philip Lee is the author of *Home Pool: The Fight to Save the Atlantic Salmon*, *Frank: The Life and Politics of Frank McKenna*, and *Bittersweet: Confessions of a Twice-Married Man*. Lee also teaches journalism at St. Thomas University in Fredericton.